Bring Your Own Sheets

Tales from a Charleston

Bed & Breakfast

Bring Your Own Sheets

Tales from a Charleston

Bed & Breakfast

BRIAN K. McGREEVY

Published in Charleston, South Carolina, by Brian K. McGreevy.

Printed in the United States of America

For Jane, Whit, Amy,

Mary Hollis, and Anne,

who lived the tales

Prologue

Was I ready to give up all this? The perfect green lawn at Lucknam Park was mottled with shadows from the dense foliage of the ancient trees surrounding the luxurious country house hotel, one of the finest in England. It was a gorgeous setting to conclude my last business trip before abandoning the corporate world. It had been a wonderful week in the U.K., replete with successful meetings with CEOs of billion dollar companies, brilliant dinners at the American Embassy in London and at Longleat, the stately home of the Marquess of Bath, and plenty of comfortable nights in the lap of luxury at the Hyde Park Hotel and Lucknam Park.

Was I ready to give this up--the expense account, the glamorous travel, the six-figure salary, the intellectual challenges, my talented and hard-working staff, the financial security of a company with piles of surplus in the bank? Well, too bad if I wasn't, because I had done it--I had caused shock and consternation by resigning from what many of my friends thought was a to-die-for dream job in order to buy a rambling 18th century house in

Charleston that we would run as a B&B. After the trip to England I would have one week back in the office before closing the deal--one week to wrap up a fifteen year career, pack up our house and kids, and move back to Charleston, the city where I grew up. Had we lost our minds, or would this be the best thing that ever happened to us?

After a wild week in the office and teary farewells to my staff, I was off to Hartsfield, the Atlanta airport, once again. During the last five years, I had developed a love/hate relationship with the airport. Having spent so much time there, I now knew every nook and cranny of the international concourse, the hundreds of different parking options, the various elite lounges and clubs--all very comfortable and all designed to make you forget that you were going to be trapped in a tin can over the ocean at the total mercy of the elements and the airline, no matter how many smiling faces were fawning upon you and no matter how many hot towels you were offered. So, it was a familiar place, and I had to admit feeling the smugness of the veteran road warrior who knows how to navigate the chaos and confusion that usually prevail at this busiest of airports. But today, it was Concourse A for the short hop to Charleston, rather than the long haul on the train to Concourse E and the exotica of international travel.

Change was definitely in the offing.

April

Arriving in Charleston, I gave a silent prayer of thanks for the tiny, efficient airport where you could actually walk 100 feet from baggage claim and be at your rental car--none of those infernal vans to the off-site rental car lots that were one of the banes of my business travel when I wasn't being met by a car and driver. No guards at baggage claim, either--in Atlanta, before you can proceed to the parking lot you always have to produce the correct slip of paper to match each article of luggage in order to satisfy the baggage guards. After a marathon international trip, this sensible anti-theft procedure that stands between you and your ability to get home to crash in your own bed can be enough to send you over the edge. With my one small bag full of cashier's checks and other documents for closing, I found my rental car and headed down the road to Charleston, our soon-to-be home.

Though Charleston is surely one of the most

beautiful cities in the world, the approaches to the city by land are all singularly unprepossessing. Billboards, fertilizer factories, ugly suburban development, and loads of cheap motels give no hint of the cultivated gem that lies where the Ashley and Cooper Rivers meet (locals would add that the Ashley and Cooper meet to form the Atlantic Ocean-- Charlestonians understand the grand role that the Creator must have intended for their fair city). As I drove through the gathering dusk into the historic district, I was awed once more by the sheer and overpowering beauty of the place. The tiniest detail of an intricate Charleston iron gate or of an ancient carved pediment speaks of a conviction that beauty elevates the soul, a dedication to the delight of craftsmanship that is intoxicating, perhaps all the more so because that dedication is mostly lost to us today.

As I parked across from the house that would become our home the next day, I marveled at our sheer good fortune to be in such an earthly paradise. The old house on King Street looked silent and a little other-worldly in the pale moonlight illuminating its facade. I thought of all the faces of those who had come upon this house and then taken it for their own--from its earliest tenants, most likely country planters renting during the pre-Revolutionary social season, to the glittering aristocracy of the early 19th century, followed by the bitter years of the Civil War and the years of tenement-style boarding in a city that fell from fabulous wealth to abject poverty virtually overnight, and the final insult of the earthquake of 1886 that robbed the house of its piazzas in front and led to a few Victorian alterations. I offered a silent prayer that our years would be among the good ones in the house's long history, which would surely go on long years after we were gone.

Following instructions from my friend Preston (who was serving as our real estate agent), I walked around to the back gate, trampled my way through the jungle that gave little signal that it had once been a formal garden, and found the house key under a flower pot. With some trepidation I began to make my way to the back door, struggling through the dark tangle of vines that caught my arms and legs at every turn. It was very dark back here, but the heady scent of tea olive was everywhere, which seemed like a good omen.

I remembered from a previous visit that somewhere under this overgrowth of vegetation were the back steps which led up to the one remaining piazza (which was really more of a porch than a grand Charleston piazza). There was a back door off the piazza, and I was sure I could feel my way along even in the dark. Feeling progressively more confident as I found the back steps and groped my way along the remains of the porch railing, I knew I should be almost to the back door. I took one more step--and suddenly plunged down into a dark abyss as the silence was broken by loud cracking sounds while the rotten wood of the porch floor collapsed around me.

Undaunted, a little shaken but otherwise uninjured upon landing (and trying not to notice the sounds of scurrying which indicated little creatures had taken up residence where I was lying), I managed to pull myself out without taking any more of the floor down with me, and hauled myself up to the back door. The key fit perfectly, and I stepped into the entry hall.

Not having been in the house for several months, and knowing it had been empty and that it needed major renovation, I had steeled myself against how bad everything might look. Despite the collapsing porch floor, the water dripping from the ceiling, the holes in the plaster, the impossible kitchen, and the dank smell of neglect, the silver moonlight poured through the windows to illuminate the soaring proportions of the drawing room and its magnificent woodwork, as well as the simple elegance of the old staircase, raising my spirits. We might be buying a ruin, but what a glorious ruin it was!

After an uneventful closing the next day, I walked out of the lawyer's office that bright April morning with the title to our own little piece of Charleston history in my portfolio, not to mention a hefty mortgage document. Now it was time to get to work on carrying out our business plan so that there would be some income to help pay that mortgage, but first we had to (a) renovate the house and (b) move all our family and possessions from Atlanta and (c) figure out how to live in the house and support our family while renovations went on around us.

With my background in business and strategic planning, I charted out what seemed to be a perfect schedule for renovating and moving and getting an income stream going. Even though somewhere in my mind I knew that the odds of staying on schedule were slim to none, it was an aid to my sanity to have something to aspire to, and I thought it might make the bank feel better about the money they had loaned us to start a venture in a business in which neither of us had any experience whatsoever.

Resolving to start well, I immediately went to work on the first thing on the schedule, which was to drive directly from the closing in North Charleston back down to the historic district and meet the painter at the house so he and his crew could get to work.

Pulling up in front of the house, I saw that Michael Gregg was already there waiting for me, dressed in his painter's whites and with his van of equipment, including what looked like at least 20 ladders of all shapes and sizes, parked on the street. Michael would prove to be one of the great blessings we discovered in the renovation process, as his smile, his faith, and his "can do' attitude helped us make it through the inevitable traumas that go along with renovating a house that was constructed in bits and pieces over three centuries. As I got out of the car, I heard music and was immediately struck by the fact that instead of hearing the typical ZZ Top, Lynrd Skynrd, or rap music pouring out of the workers' van, I was hearing what sounded like church praise music.

"What's that music you've got going over there, Michael?"

"Mr. Brian, that's some worship music. You know I got a little church where I minister on the weekend. "

"So you're a painter and a minister too?"

"That's right. You've got to thank God for Jesus every day!"

I was thanking God that we had someone who seemed like an honest, dependable painter. I would learn that Michael was not only honest and dependable, but that he was also a true craftsman with a genius for fixing old plaster as well. He also had a delightful habit of lapsing back to old Gullah expressions from time to time that I remembered hearing as a boy, especially "That be fuh true," an emphatic way of agreeing with someone.

"Michael, the walls in this room are in really bad shape."

"Umm, umm, that be fuh true."

I explained to Michael that the plan was that in two

8

weeks' time, the moving vans would arrive with all our worldly possessions, and that the main house interior had to be completely finished by that time so that we could move all the furniture in. Despite the holes in the plaster in the walls and ceilings, the grimy paint on the moldings that needed to be stripped, and the missing moldings and trim that needed to be repaired or replaced throughout all three and one-half stories of the house, Michael smiled and shook my hand.

With a twinkle in his eye, he said "Don't you worry about a thing, Mr. Brian. We'll have everything ready for you when you come."

How I hoped he was right....

Getting back in the car to head to the airport, I mentally rehearsed the other key steps in the plan. Since the house had ten bedrooms, six in the main house and four in the kitchen house, we had decided we would live in the main house with the children in three bedrooms on the third floor, our room on the upper part of the second floor, two guestrooms in a wing on the lower part of the second floor, and four guestrooms in the kitchen house. Since the main house needed paint, plaster, and a new kitchen, office, and laundry room--but no major structural work--we would get its interior finished, except for the kitchen, and move all the furniture for the whole place into the main house two weeks after closing.

We would then do the structural work on the kitchen house, renovate the kitchen house rooms, and move the furniture into them as each room was finished. We would have the two main house guestrooms ready for guests two days after moving in, hoping to attract some of the crowds in town for the Spoleto Festival, a world-renowned performing and visual arts festival that takes over Charleston's historic district in late May and early June each year.

Upon my return to Atlanta, it was time to start packing. We had acquired some extra furniture and antiques from family members for the B&B, all of which was piled in our basement in Atlanta. We tried to figure out what would go to which room in the new house but it wasn't always easy to know what would fit where, and all items that didn't have a certain destination would go to the kitchen for the time being. To preserve the mental health of our children, we decided that I would go with the moving truck to Charleston, along with a few intrepid friends, get everything settled and moved in and the children's rooms set up, and then the family and the dog would follow a month later after stays with various friends in Atlanta.

With each box label and the sound of packing tape being pressed down tightly on the seams of boxes, the reality of this impending change grew more and more evident, and the possibility of going back to our old and secure way of life grew increasingly remote. The fantasy was about to become reality. It was going to be a year to remember!

May

Before we knew it, moving day was upon us. It was time to bid farewell to Buckhead and security and say hello to Charleston and our new adventure. Since the rest of my family was staying put in Atlanta until we were sure the Charleston house would be habitable for them, I had recruited some long-suffering friends, Ryan, Jack, Steve, and Ken, to help me manage the move-in. I had called Michael Gregg on his cell phone and he had assured me everything would be done in time for the movers. Ryan and I packed our Volvo station wagon to the gills and went on to Charleston, to be followed by my other friends and the movers. When we arrived, I was delighted to discover that the main house was indeed finished inside and that all the new plaster and paint looked great.

After a small skirmish with the city authorities over getting a permit for the moving van to come down our street, the movers arrived around 8 a.m. and started unloading. Having two houses with entrances on different streets made things interesting in terms of telling the movers where everything should go, but we hoped for the best and figured we could move things later once it was all inside. We elected to put as much of the antique furniture as we could in the main house to protect it from the renovations commencing on the kitchen house, but soon realized some things would have to go to the kitchen house because we were running out of room. Ryan appointed himself chief box organizer in the kitchen and soon had the room packed like a moving van with boxes all the way to the ceiling.

Our idea was to get the drawing room, dining room, entrance hall, and two upstairs guest rooms ready and looking great, and we figured we could keep everything else closed off so that guests would not know we weren't even really moved in. Of course, the hundreds of broken-down boxes on the back porch were a bit of a giveaway, but we thought we would just keep people away from the back door and the garden, especially since the word "garden" was still aspirational at this point—"jungle" would have been more descriptive.

As the day wore on, it got progressively hotter and more humid, and we and the movers consumed massive quantities of Gatorade. Our first real hitch came when we tried to move in some furniture that was supposed to go on the second floor of the kitchen house. The kitchen house, built in the early 18th century, was very long on charm, especially with its tiny cypress stairhall and narrow stair where you had to duck your head if you were over 5' 2". We soon nicknamed this the "Stairway of Death," because when you came downstairs you would smash your forehead from nose to scalp on the lintel board. It reminded me of the story we had heard at one of the Loire Valley chateaux about one of the kings of France who was hurrying down a similar staircase, albeit more ancient and made of stone, and smashed his forehead with such force that he died from the blow.

Determined not to lose any movers or any of my friends, I had put ribbons up to mark the most dangerous spot, but it had never occurred to me to measure the hall and stair to see whether our furniture would fit. I knew we were in trouble when the movers came to tell me that there was a chair stuck on the staircase. I went to investigate, and discovered that there was indeed a leather wing chair wedged into the staircase that wouldn't budge. Eventually, with a lot of pushing and shoving and the aid of a screwdriver to remove the rail of the stairs, we were able to liberate the chair, but that left us perplexed as to what we would do with the sofa, king mattress and box springs, and two large mahogany beds that had to go up there. We concluded that our best bet was going to be the balcony on the second floor, where part of the railing was loose. We took the railing down, backed up the pick-up truck that belonged to one of my friends, and established three hoisting stations—one group to lift furniture from the ground to the truck, another to lift it from the truck almost to the level of the balcony, and a third to lean off the balcony, grab the furniture, and haul it up onto the second floor. Fortunately, this system worked pretty well and the furniture got where it needed to go without major injury to the furniture or the hoisters.

As sundown approached, we had almost finished, and we ordered a large quantity of pizza from Domino's for the movers and my friends. It was an interesting first dinner party in the new house—14 sweaty, burly, dead-tired men of various races sitting in an elegant 18th century dining room with a mahogany table and crystal chandelier, eating pizza off shreds of cardboard boxes. There wasn't much conversation because we were too exhausted and dehydrated, but there was definitely plenty of unspoken male bonding --we had all met the challenges of the day and survived by depending on one another.

Once the movers had gone, my friends and I moved to the next challenge, which was getting the entrance hall, downstairs public rooms, and the two guestrooms ready. After a few hours, we had all the furniture in the right place in those rooms, the beds and mattresses set up in the guestrooms, and the paintings and other art work ready to hang. And here we met our next challenge—hanging art in a house where the walls are not plumb and where there are no right angles at corners. Sloping ceilings, sloping floors, and sloping walls made it a real adventure to hang each piece of art, not to mention the challenge of getting nails, screws, and other hanging devices to anchor in the plaster walls without crashing to the floor and pulling large chunks of the wall out at the same time that the frame and glass shattered in a million pieces on the floor. I soon realized that my little six foot ladder was of virtually no use when hanging art in a room with 15' ceilings. By standing on furniture, standing on each other's shoulders, and scaling fireplace mantels, we eventually got most of the art up and looking fairly straight. The next order of business was cleaning up the floors in the guest rooms, where there was a good bit of splattered paint on the hardwood floors. Steve, Ken, and Jack took this on, getting on their hands and knees and scrubbing, while Ryan and I went to the kitchen to try to unbox essentials. The kitchen had several hundred boxes piled three high up to the ceiling, with narrow alleys in between. We quickly realized that it was going to take weeks to get all this stuff unpacked and because the task was not unlike the labors of Hercules, we soon christened the kitchen the Aegean Stables. Finally, around 2 a.m., we called it quits for the night and slept wherever we could find a spot.

The next day, we had a quick breakfast and went to early church at St. Philip's, seeking divine assistance in finishing our tasks. Things went smoothly that afternoon, and by 4 o'clock, the beds were made, there were towels in the guestrooms, and the public rooms downstairs looked great. We felt like master illusionists—the rest of the house looked like London after the Blitz, but who would ever know besides us? I bid a fond farewell to my friends, who had to drive back to Atlanta to be at their real jobs the next day. They had worked uncomplainingly night and day all weekend at hard, hot, wrenching labor with no thought of reward. Waving as they drove off down King Street back to Atlanta and what had been my world for 15 years, I reflected that I was truly blessed to have such friends. A bit misty-eyed, I turned back to the house and my one remaining project—changing out one window unit air conditioner, which I had assured my friends I could handle on my own so they could get on the road. How hard could it be, right?

One of the things that had somehow escaped our notice when we were looking at the house before we bought it was that the third floor, for all its charming 18th century arched windows and beautiful wide original floorboards and stunning views across the Charleston rooftops, was missing something really important that we had taken for granted in every other house we had ever looked at—heating and air conditioning. We had naively assumed that the old (and broken) window unit air conditioner up there was just to provide "booster power" on really hot days, since we were right under the roof. As I prepared for the children's arrival, I had very quickly became aware that there was no air conditioning, and then as I looked it became apparent that it was worse than I thought—there was no ductwork, no vents, no heating system, no anything. Baseboards and ceilings were completely intact and vent-free. For whatever reason, the previous owners had installed central heat and air and all the requisite ductwork on the first two floors, but left the third floor out completely. I suppose one could look at it and say that the third floor offered an "authentic" experience of 18th century Charleston—i.e., that you would endure heat in the summertime that could fry an egg on the floor or melt your jewelry—but that kind of authenticity was something that I was not sure our children would really appreciate.

Upon consultation with several contractors, it had quickly become apparent that there was a reason the central heat and air had stopped with the second floor—there was virtually no way to put it in without major league remodeling (moving walls, moving the staircase, eliminating the only closet, and other bad options). There was not room for ductwork, and even if there had been, an untold amount of 18th and 19th century plaster and woodwork would have to be disturbed. There was no place to put the blower. There was no way to run the drain lines in a way that we could be sure would avoid leakage or mold problems elsewhere in the house. It appeared, though, that one or two strong window units that provided both heat and air conditioning might do the trick, at least in the short term, while we evaluated what our options might be.

So, off I had gone to the appliance store, and $1000 later, I was heaving into the back of my Volvo station wagon an absolutely enormous box with a hugely powerful window unit that would provide both heat and air conditioning, and I left it in the back of the car while we worked on getting the "guest" part of the house ready.

Once I had waved goodbye to my friends, I realized the first challenge before me was to carry this enormous box up three and a half stories worth of stairs. There was no one around to help me, so I decided I would just do it myself. I was still reasonably young and in reasonably good shape, right? So, up I went. The first flight of stairs went pretty well, but then I had to stop to rest and catch my breath. My Brooks Brothers shirt was getting pretty wet from the strain-induced perspiration, so I took a moment to change to an old Sea Island t-shirt, figuring I could visualize being at the Beach Club at the

Cloister and perhaps slow down my racing heart. As I bent down and hoisted the box again, I felt a little twinge in my back but pressed on anyway, heaving the box up and mounting the next section of stairs. Here things began to get more interesting, as after the turn in the stairs the staircase became much narrower and the open banister gave way to a plaster wall on one side. I hoisted and pushed and shoved but soon realized the box was stuck, firmly wedged between an 18th century handrail (which was making alarming groaning noises as I had pushed it several inches out of plumb) and an 18th century plaster wall that was like granite.

The one advantage was that the box was so firmly wedged I could let go of it and contemplate my situation, alternating between feeling consternation and then visualizing myself on the chaise longue at Sea Island, as I tried to calm down my heart rate. Eventually, my worry that I was going to destroy the stair handrail outweighed my concern for shoving the box on up to the next part of the stairs, so I decided that I would just take the unit out of the box. How hard could it be to open a box?

Well, I will pass over the details of being impaled on three-inch long sharp copper staples, receiving paper cuts from the instruction cards in the box, and using my last strength to break open six-inch thick Styrofoam blocks to free the unit, as well as the cries of agony when the several hundred pound unit slipped and landed on the top part of my foot—let's just focus on the positive, which is that the unit would now fit up the stairs. Now I was visualizing the chaise longue and an icy beverage and the murmur of the ocean in the background just to keep myself going.

Making one last heave, I got the unit up in the air again and pushed forward up the last section of stairs and made it through the door to the platform that had formerly held a bathtub. The previous owners did not have air conditioning up here, but they had built a platform and installed a claw-footed tub in the middle of the bedroom— all I could think is maybe you were supposed to fill it up with ice and sit in it when the heat became unbearable. I preferred my visualizing the chaise longue at the beach club.

Now that I was sure that the worst was over, I considered what I would need to install the new unit. I had measured the window beforehand to ensure everything would fit, and made sure we had the right electrical outlet with the right type of socket. So, all that remained to be done was to swap out the old non-functioning unit for the new one, and then I could enjoy the delights of Arctic breezes in the sweltering heat. Alas, nothing is ever as easy as it seems it should be. When I tried to lift the window sash in order to remove the old unit, which had no evident bolts, it would not budge. I looked in vain for nails or bolts or pegs or anything that could be holding the window down. I went all the way downstairs and got the tool for opening windows that are painted shut and went all the way around the perimeter of the sash, thinking that was the problem, and then tried lifting again. If anything, the sash seemed more firmly stuck. My visualizing of the Beach Club at the Cloister wasn't really working for me anymore, and I was getting pretty annoyed. It had been nearly three hours since I began working on this air conditioner installation, and to be thwarted by a stuck window was incredibly frustrating. I decided to try a few more angled heaves at the sash, and then I was going to go back downstairs for the crowbar, and too bad about the 18th century woodwork around the window. I wanted that window unit in, and I wanted it in NOW. Summoning all the strength I could, I gave another heave, and with a loud cracking sound, the window sash flew all the way up and a microsecond later the old window unit was not only freed up, but it was airborne!

It had never occurred to me to notice that the old unit was sitting at a funny angle and to realize that the sash wouldn't open because the full weight of the old unit was leaning against it, ready to fall outside the house whenever someone came to liberate it. After another microsecond of exultation that the window was finally open and my task nearly complete, my exultation turned to horror and terror. I realized that the window was right over the sidewalk and that several hundred pounds of metal with sharp corners were now hurtling down, possibly onto the heads of some unsuspecting tourists or into the windshield of an automobile or onto the roof of a carriage tour or the horses pulling it, any of which could not escape an almost certain death if they were in the wrong spot. Visions of carnage and lawsuits replaced the chaise longue in my head, as I leaned out the window screaming:

"LOOK OUT below! FORE!"

"Hit the decks! INCOMING!"

Moments later, I saw the old air conditioner hit the sidewalk, bounce in the air, and land again on the sidewalk with a wheeze and a crash, crumpled up like an old accordion. Thanks be to God, there were no people on the sidewalk at all, and miraculously the street was empty of both cars and carriage tours. So far as I knew, there were no witnesses to what could have been fatal stupidity on my part, and murmuring a prayer of thanks, I ran downstairs and hoisted the remains of the air conditioner into a box and hid it in the garbage enclosure. Newly energized by this deliverance from disaster, I bounded back upstairs, secured the new unit in the window, plugged it in, hit the switch, and was rewarded by.... silence. Nothing happened—nada—rien. Surely this was not just, after all I had been through. Perhaps this was some kind of existential innkeeper purgatory; it was certainly hot enough. Muttering under my breath, I went downstairs to check the circuit breaker.

Like many things in an old house, checking the circuit breaker is far more complex than it sounds. In our case, the three different electrical panels from the various systems in the house were all located in the utility/laundry room, which seems logical. Unfortunately, they were located on the wall behind the upright freezer and the stacked washer/dryer unit, which made them not only virtually inaccessible but also impossible to see. In order to get to the breaker box, you had to get the small ladder, climb up to the top of the upright freezer, and shimmy across the top on your stomach. Because there was a shelf overhead that blocked all the light, you also had to have a flashlight with you. Next, trying to maintain your balance so you did not fall six feet to the floor or slip off and get wedged behind the appliances, you had to drop both arms over the back of the freezer, opening the breaker box with one hand while shining the flashlight with the other, all the while trying not to knock into the dryer vent that went across the gap and which would come loose at the slightest prod, blowing hot lint into your face. Meanwhile, you had to pray that it was not one of the bottom four breakers, which could only be reached by someone with the armspan of an orangutan, and required you to get back down off the freezer and get a broomstick to use to hit at them and hope you could knock them back into position. Fortunately, this time it was one of the top breakers, so I flipped it back into position and prayed that I could manage to lift myself off the freezer and back onto the ladder, now that my back was racked with uncontrollable spasms and all my other muscles were quivering like jelly from overexertion. I slid back down to the ladder, walked over to the stairs, and slowly pulled myself up the banister for the three and a half floor journey to the new air conditioner.

The moment of truth had arrived. I turned the switch, thinking that if it didn't work this time, I might be the next thing jumping out the window. Glory hallelujah, the click of the switch was followed by the blessed sound of air gushing into the machine, the fan running at top speed, and moments later blasts of cold air sweeter than water to a man dying of thirst flooded across my face. Who needs to try to climb Mount Everest to prove yourself, when you can run the third floor air conditioner installation gauntlet in the "comfort" of your own home?

I decided that was enough for one day. It was starting to get dark, and I was completely worn out, but had that feeling of intense satisfaction that comes on those days when you know you have really gotten a lot done. I was ready for my first night alone in my new home.

One of the wonderful things about Charleston is that it is a city rich in sounds. As I awoke early the next morning, the sun was streaming in the windows and the air was filled with the sound of birds, not just a few twitters here and there, but a whole chorus. The breeze was ruffling the leaves of the ancient live oaks, and the venerable chimes of St. Michael's Church were announcing that it was fifteen minutes before the next hourly chime. Early in the morning, it is easy to feel transported back to another, earlier Charleston, a Charleston without cars, iPhones, and FedEx, where life proceeded at a more languid pace. This sense of being suspended in time is one of the chief lures of Charleston's beauty, and the city's sounds—the cry of gulls, the lapping of waves at the Battery, the singing of countless birds, and the chimes of ancient bells—are a constant music from the past that plays in the background of our modern lives.

Against all odds, we were on schedule. It was the last week of the Spoleto Festival, and our two B&B rooms were ready, and inside the house the only parts the guests could see looked beautiful, as the chaos and construction were all behind closed doors. The initial preparations were all done. The next step was before us: our first guests!

June

Running a successful B&B requires not only that you have a beautiful property and warm hospitality, but also that people actually choose to come stay with you. It was Monday morning in Charleston, and I had a brand new B&B with two guestrooms ready for guests to come. Since it was still Spoleto season, I was hopeful we could attract some last-minute guests to come stay with us. I called the Visitors Center and several B&B reservations agencies to let them know we had rooms available, and was thrilled that within a couple of hours both rooms had been booked for the next two nights.

As I double-checked the guestrooms to make sure all was as it should be, the doorbell rang and I came downstairs to answer it. Opening the front door was a bit of a challenge. In Charleston, the older something is, the more reverence it is due, and our front door was old indeed and hence worthy of great reverence. It still had the old lockbox from the early 1800s, plus a new deadbolt. Opening the door demanded a precise alignment not unlike a planetary conjunction whereby one knob had to be turned just so far, so that the catch lined up with the very small opening on the lock box, while at the same time the deadbolt was turned back with just the right amount of pressure applied so that the bolt wouldn't stick, and while all these precise machinations were occurring, the door had to be pulled back with a strong tug at just the right time so that it would pop the hermetic seal caused by the swelling of anything made of wood, a result of Charleston's ubiquitous humidity that often rivals that of the African rain forest.

After several tugs, I finally got the door open and found Michael Gregg waiting for me, a smile on his face as always.

"Mr. Brian, this place is lookin' good for sure. Will it suit you for us to be workin' on the outside today? "

"Thanks, Michael, that would be great. What's going on with the gutters?"

"Well, sir, that gutter man you got, he *said* he's comin' today, so I can go on and take off the old gutters if you want."

There was a certain portentous cocking of the head and narrowing of the eyes when Michael talked about the gutter man which didn't come right out and say he was trouble, but which led me to think there might be more to the gutter man than met the eye.

"That sounds good. Just be careful, because we've got some guests coming in today."

"Yes sir, that's just great you already got folks comin'. The Lord's gonna take care of you—you just keep trusting in Him."

Thanking Michael for his encouragement, I went to the kitchen to see what I could unearth not only to serve *for* breakfast but to serve breakfast *on* the next morning. After a few hours of digging through boxes, I had managed to find plates, silver flatware, and glasses, plus placemats and napkins. We had already thought through menus for offering a full, hot breakfast once we were fully operational, but in the meantime we had decided to do a continental breakfast. I wasn't quite set up for cooking yet since I couldn't find the box with the pots and pans, though I had managed to unearth the coffee maker. A trip to the local bakery provided me with some delectable pastries, which I rounded out with some fresh fruit. I figured presented properly it would be plenty for the continental breakfast we were advertising.

One of the great tricks of running a good B&B is trying to figure out when your guests will actually arrive. This question is important for several reasons. If you are the only host, you want to make sure you are there to greet the guests and help them get settled, but at the same time you also need to be able to go to the grocery store, run errands, work with the contractor, get things set up with reservations agencies, and so on. Not being able to be two places at once is a real handicap in the B&B business. Another reason you want to know when people are arriving is so you can ensure that their room has been thoroughly cleaned and is all ready for them when they arrive. You also don't want to offer current guests late checkout if there are people arriving for their room at lunchtime. It is amazing how guests don't seem to understand that if checkout time is at 11 a.m., it is pretty unlikely that they will be able to get into their room at 10 a.m. and find it perfectly beautiful and spotlessly clean. I wanted to make sure that I was there to greet our very first guests, so I made it a priority to be back at the house by 10 a.m. and waiting in the Drawing Room for the guests to arrive.

In Charleston, the Drawing Room is a term of art for what in other places might be called a living room, a parlor, or a sitting room. A Drawing Room in fact has nothing whatsoever to do with painting or drawing or any kind of visual art, but it refers to an art of a type even more important in Charleston history—the art of gracious living as expressed through civilized conversation. "Drawing" is a familiar derivation from "Withdrawing," and the rooms so named are those to which gentlemen and ladies would withdraw after dinner for conversation. In grand houses or those of a certain pretension, after dinner the gentlemen would withdraw to one room to enjoy their wine, to smoke, and to discuss politics and literature, while the ladies would withdraw to another room to do needlework, to discuss music, and to comment on the latest fashions. Whether in fact these roles and topics of conversation were strictly observed and whether the atmosphere was so rarefied and refined as Charleston ladies of a certain age would like us to believe remain a matter for conjecture and speculation today, but surely in a place of hospitality such as we envisioned creating, we would aspire to the aforementioned "art of gracious living as expressed through civilized conversation."

Regardless of whether our conversation could be termed civilized, we certainly had the right kind of space for it. The Drawing Room was easily the most spectacular room of the house. About twenty-five feet square with fifteen-foot ceilings, the room was awash with light all day long from its six magnificent windows, two on each exterior wall. Each window was over ten feet tall and was surrounded by some of the best hand-carved Regency gougework in the city of Charleston, which matched the fine Regency carving on the mantel of the fireplace and on the door surrounds. Imposing double doors on enormous hinges original to the house led into the Drawing Room, but all this Regency splendor was broken up by a later Victorian ceiling that was installed after the original ceiling collapsed. In the Charleston of my childhood, "Victorian" was synonymous with "tacky", "bad taste", and "nouveau riche;" as most "nice" families did not have the means after the War Between the States to appropriate Victorian style through remodeling or new building, they simply rejected the style as being gaudy and inappropriate.

One fortunate consequence of this stylistic snobbery was that many of the gems of Charleston's colonial and Adam architecture were preserved in their original condition. Some houses, however, especially those damaged significantly in the 1886 earthquake like ours, sported anomalous Victorian alterations which to my mind frequently made them somewhat warmer and less forbidding, in the same way a favorite prim and proper great-aunt might seem more approachable when wearing a crocheted shawl of a particularly garish color. The Victorian ceiling in our Drawing Room was erected at the same time as a fireplace brick surround of cerulean blue was installed between the Regency mantel and the iron insert that converted the fireplace to coal-burning. The ceiling and the bright blue brick seemed to say "Come on in—we needn't take ourselves TOO seriously!"

The front windows of the Drawing Room, with their vast expanses of wavy 19th century glass, overlooked the Miles Brewton House across the street, easily the most famous house in Charleston and one of the best examples of Georgian architecture in America. Regarded as the finest house in the city since its construction in 1765, the house had been commandeered by the British to serve as their headquarters after they took Charleston in the Revolutionary War, and Lord Clinton and Lord Rawdon, along with their frequent visitor Cornwallis, plotted much of the Southern strategy for the British in this house, then owned by Rebecca Brewton Motte, one of the great heroines of the Revolutionary War. Her granddaughter, Elizabeth Alston, would one day become the mistress of our house, which she received as a wedding present from her father, Col. William Alston, upon her marriage to Senator Arthur Hayne. Arthur and Elizabeth Hayne were the ones who around 1830 added this grand Drawing Room to the earlier 18th century portion of our house. In 1865, the Union troops who took the city from the Confederates once again claimed the Miles Brewton house as the headquarters for their commanding officers. Though all its history, the Miles Brewton house has never left the ownership of the descendants of Rebecca Brewton Motte.

As I gazed out the window and mused on the glorious history of these two houses set like old friends across from one another, I noticed a curious site on the sidewalk down the block. The thing that had first attracted my attention was sunlight reflecting off the bright gold metallic spandex jumpsuit and big jewelry worn by a woman with an enormous pompadour of bright red hair. The woman, whose breadth was such that the jumpsuit strained mightily at its buttons, was carrying several coolers and had unimaginably long fingernails painted bright orange to match her toenails. Her companion looked like he was attired for a skit about tacky tourists from the North, as he sported dark plaid shorts, a white undershirt rolled up at the sleeves, long black nylon socks that nearly reached his knees, and brown sandals. His very pale skin contrasted vividly with his thick black glasses and his gold neckchains. He too was carrying a collection of coolers.

Wondering what in the world this over-the-top duo was doing in our neighborhood, I was reminded of the paid advertisement I had just noticed in the Charleston *Post & Courier* that very morning, something that I thought could only happen in Charleston. The advertisement, taken out by several of our neighbors of my parents' generation, read:

Dear Visitor to Charleston: As you enjoy our lovely and historic city, her ancient monuments and houses of worship, we ask that you show respect, as we are certain you would at home, by wearing appropriate clothing at all times. Bare chests, tank tops, short shorts, spandex, and bare feet are not considered to be correct attire in the historic district. Thank your cooperation.
Charleston Citizens for Sartorial Rectitude

Apparently, there was increasing concern in the neighborhood that inappropriately-clad (or should I say UN-clad) tourists were marring the beauty of the historic district, and there was a lot of whispering that Charleston

34

was getting the sort of visitors who really ought to have gone to Myrtle Beach instead.

Gazing at these two specimens out the window as they walked up King Street, I thought perhaps they were part of a promotion organized by the people who ran the ad as an example of what NOT to wear, and that perhaps the coolers were for a lemonade stand to get people to stop and to help draw attention to the cause of better-dressed tourists. As they progressed up the block, I was surprised to see them stop in front of our house, and even more surprised when the gold-jumpsuited woman rang the doorbell.

"Oh no," I thought. "They must be lost or needing directions. I need to get them out of here before our guests arrive."

I opened the door, smiled, and said in my nicest voice "May I help you?"

The gold jumpsuited woman, coolers held in front of her like a battering ram, knocked me out of the way and muscled her way into the entrance hall, followed by the man, and announced "Well, Howie, this must be it." What a place, huh? Jeesh."

Somewhat alarmed, I smiled again at her and said "May I help you?"

Fixing me with a baleful stare, she replied "You work in this joint?"

"Yes ma'am," I replied.

(As my mind raced, groping for an explanation of what these people were doing here, I finally seized upon it—it must be a practical joke. Either my parents or some of my former staff at my old company must have decided to hire these people to imitate the guests from hell to give me a laugh on our first day of being open for business. I figured I would play along.)

Stomping her foot, she announced "Well, we ain't got all day, do we Howie? Show us the room, mister—right now! I need to take a load off."

Smiling politely, I inquired "And do you have a reservation, ma'am?"

Putting her hands on her hips, she pointed her finger at my face and said "Don't you get smart with me, mister. Do you think I would be at a joint like this if I couldda found a room reservation anywhere else? That broad at the bed and breakfast agency said she called you and it was all fixed. The name is RUEDD."

Horrified, I realized that was indeed the name of the guests who were supposed to occupy the Wisteria Room, while I simultaneously tried to restrain myself from bursting into hysterical laughter about the appropriateness of the woman's name. Mustering my diplomatic skills, I said "Please follow me upstairs. Your room is all ready for you. May I help you with your...um...things?"

"Don't you touch my coolers! Howie and I are the ONLY people allowed to touch them. Got it, buster?"

"Certainly, ma'am," I replied as we reached the top of the stairs and the entrance to the room. Opening the door, I announced cheerfully "Here is the Wisteria Room. I know you will enjoy it."

Sun streamed through the six windows of the room, illuminating the beautiful 18th century heart pine floors and the elegant Georgian mantelpiece. A 19th century blue and tan Chinese rug from my wife's family sat between the four-poster mahogany rice bed and an elegant Federal mahogany dresser from my mother's family's plantation. Fresh flowers adorned the bedside tables, on which sat elegant alabaster lamps that had been my great-aunt's. An original etching of St. Michael's Church by Elizabeth O'Neill Verner, one of the most revered artists of the Charleston Renaissance of the 1930s and 1940s, hung over the mantel. The new premium mattresses were made up with hand-ironed all cotton sheets and topped with a beautiful comforter that was an authentic reproduction of an 18th century botanical pattern from Winterthur. The freshly painted walls were a pale violet color which contrasted appealingly with the big white baseboards and white cotton floor length curtains and swags. My grandmother's Chinese floral teacups adorned the mantel, flanked by brass candleholders with ivory candles and hurricane shades on each side. The room looked stunningly beautiful, comfortable, and inviting.

As Mrs. Ruedd entered the room, I saw a look of shock on her face and then she exclaimed "OH...MY...GOD!"

Thinking she was overwhelmed by the beauty of it all, I said "It's lovely, isn't it?"

Staring at me, she exclaimed "Why do you got all this old foynitchuh (*Ed. Note: furniture*)--can't you uhfowuhd (*Ed. Note: afford*) anything new? And do you even got electricity in this joint? What's the deal with putting us in here with all dese candles?

I explained as nicely as I could while my blood pressure was skyrocketing "This old furniture is all antique and part of the experience of staying in an historic bed and breakfast. And yes, there is electricity. It seems, though, that we are not offering what you expected, and I would be happy to try to find you another place to stay."

"Humph," she said. "Get out for a minute and let me talk to Howie."

As I left the room, she slammed the door behind me. My mind raced to think of how I could get rid of them. The agency that sent them marketed itself as "Ensuring a perfect match: your property and the kinds of guests you want paired with just the right clientele from our pool of discerning guests." Obviously there had been a mistake somewhere. Maybe I could...

The door opened suddenly. "Hey you," she said. "Get in here. We decided we think we can stand it since it's only two nights. And I got you figured out. I got a friend back home that collects old Coca-Cola bottles. Drinks 'em but can't make herself throw 'em away. Piles of 'em all over the house. Just like you and all this old junk you got all over this joint."

Maybe we didn't need a Drawing Room after all....

July

Having survived the trials of the Ruedd guests, we were ready for anything, and were happily surprised after that inauspicious start to find most of our guests pleasant and interesting. Since we do a lavish breakfast in the formal dining room where guests have to talk with one another, it is gratifying to see conversations and bonhomie develop among guests who have not previously known one another. We try to create a setting that makes guests feel like they are in a private Charleston home, being treated to a special and elegant breakfast.

The dining room features mahogany early 19th century Federal family antiques and is painted a sunny yellow, which shows off the gleaming white 18th century woodwork and the red, yellow, and blue Mario Buatta chintz curtains. The large dining table is set on an old Chinese red oriental rug, and on the table are French placemats and linen napkins. Each place is set with sterling silver flatware, Waterford crystal goblets, and English porcelain china. Fresh flowers abound, and there are beautiful views of neighboring historic homes from the five large windows that grace the room.

One of the benefits of having a bed and breakfast is the chance to get to know people from all over the world, and a leisurely breakfast was a great opportunity for us to connect with our guests. Generally, people who want to stay in a B&B rather than a hotel are people who are interested in getting to know local culture and the insider's view of what a place is like, and who also are interested in having interaction with the hosts and other guests. On good days, the conversation at breakfast is like that at a particularly good dinner party where one meets new people with whom one feels an instant affinity and the room is full of conviviality and positive energy. Then, there are those other days, fortunately few and far between, when we are desperately trying to make conversation among guests with very little in common.

This month's most difficult breakfast involved six guests--a former official for the U.S Centers for Disease Control (familiarly known as the CDC) who was now a medical school professor and noted author and columnist, his "lady friend" (a polite Southern term for a woman with whom a man is cohabiting without benefit of clergy); a carpenter from south Georgia and his wife, who were salt of the earth folks but not highly educated; and three guests from Finland who spoke no English and could apparently say only three words:

1. "Ja",
2. "TING-oo"(thank you), and
3. "Coffee".

Let's listen in as I serve as host for this unlikely menage:

Wife of Carpenter to Finns: "Whar are y'all frum?"

Finns: (putting heads together, frantic whispering, then hesitantly) "Coffee?"

Wife: "No thank yew. What I said was (almost shouting) WHAR (pause...)ARE (pause...)Y'ALL (pause...) FRUM!?!"

Finns: (whispering and desperate looks to Host)"Ting-oo"

Host (quick-witted as usual): "They're from Finland. I don't think they speak English."

Finns: "Ting-oo"

Wife: "Humph. Furriners. (turning her gaze to doctor) "Whar are Y'ALL frum?"

Doctor: "I'm from Cambridge and she's from New York."

Wife: "So y'all are YANKEES but not from the same place! Isn't that ....interestin'...Well, well, well..."

Finns: (whispering, looking at coffee)

Host (seeing that the Rebel flag was about to be raised): "Dr. X is an expert who used to work for the CDC and focused on health problems in the Third World."

Wife: "Well, well, well... Thard World. Idn't that whar that flesh-eating disease thang wuz?"

Doctor: "Do you mean the Ebola virus?"

Wife: "Yeah, that ee-BOWL-ah thang. Makes yore skin ooze and turn black afore it rots and you die."

Finns: (whispering, nodding, exchange glances, then all put hands in lap in unison)

Husband from Georgia (looking with distress at the sausages on his plate): "Ah thank ah'm going' back to mah room."

On days like this, one is tempted to clear all the food out early to make sure that the guests leave breakfast before any new controversy can break out.

Other breakfast high drama can result from people's quirks about food. Perhaps because breakfast is the first meal of a new day, many people seem to have a routine for breakfast, and breaking that routine can cause great trauma. We try to be accommodating as we can but will admit to having seen some quirky things. Coffee is always a good starting place for quirks. The Esthers, two elderly ladies from Brooklyn both named (you guessed it) Esther, loved to send back the just-brewed coffee to be re-heated every morning. Each morning we would wait with baited breath to see what the day's judgment on the coffee would be, as we poured coffee that had only been out of the brewer for 30 seconds, and each day we were rewarded with "Oh no, dear. This coffee has gotten cold. In New York we like our coffee HOT. Get your girl in the kitchen to reheat this. I can't drink COLD coffee." So we would dutifully take the coffee back to the kitchen, pour a fresh cup, and microwave it until it was scalding. We had to be very careful bringing it back in, though, for fear of a lawsuit if it should spill on anyone. We weren't ready to join McDonald's on the list of places being sued because their coffee was too hot.

Another memorable breakfast involved a delightful family from Australia with two very cute children who were 8 and 10 years old. The children responded very politely to the other guests' requests for them to "say something in Australian" ("Good day, mate/How's the shrimp on the barbie?" etc.) and then came into breakfast with a large jar of Vegemite. For those of you who are not among the culinary cognoscenti, Vegemite is a, shall we say, *unique* food product that is found in Australia.

To quote from the Wikipedia entry on Vegemite:

Vegemite (pronounced "VEH-gee-mite", IPA: [ˈvɛdʒɪˌmaɪt]) is the registered brand name for a dark brown, salty food paste mainly used as a spread on sandwiches and toast, though occasionally used in cooking. Popular in Australia and New Zealand—Vegemite is semi-jokingly called one of Australia's national foods—it is seldom found elsewhere. Food technologist Dr. Cyril P. Callister invented Vegemite in 1923 when his employer, the Australian Fred Walker Company, had him develop a spread from Brewer'sYeast. Vegemite's current name was picked at random out of a hat by Fred Walker's daughter, Sheilah. The name reflects the use of vegetable and yeast extract as compared to the beef and yeast extract that Marmite is made from. Vegemite's taste and manufacture are similar to the British Marmite - although vegemite is somewhat saltier - and indeed the product was for a short

44

time known as "Parwill" as a pun on Marmite's name (as in the sentence: **"Marmite** not like the taste, but I'm sure **Parwill"**).

However this attempt to compete with Marmite's growing share of the market was unsuccessful and the name was changed back to Vegemite. Today Vegemite far outsells Marmite and other similar spreads in both Australia and New Zealand. The brand is now owned by Kraft Foods, an American multinational that is part of the Phillip Morris tobacco company in the Altria Group of companies.While highly popular in Australia and New Zealand, it has never been successfully marketed elsewhere. It is notorious for the dislike it generates amongst some foreigners, particularly Americans. Note that Vegemite is not liked by *all* Australians - many find it far too salty to be palatable - but it remains an iconic symbol of Australia.

Vegemite is often spread with liberal amounts of butter to help to soften the strong taste, or with sliced or melted cheese. It is also a key ingredient in the popular "Cheesymite Scroll" or "Cheddarmite Scroll" produced by bakeries in Australia, a savoury spiral pastry which includes cheese spread and vegemite. Vegemite's rise to popularity was helped by marketing campaigns in the 1940s, using groups of smiling, attractive healthy children singing a catchy jingle entitled "We're happy little Vegemites". Indeed, many Australians still use the phrase "happy little Vegemite" to describe such children. Re-edited versions of the advertisements and jingle continue to be used for their appeal to patriotic nostalgia.--*Wikipedia contributors. "Vegemite." Wikipedia, The Free Encyclopedia. Wikipedia, The Free Encyclopedia, 15 Feb. 2013. Web. 18 Feb. 2013.*

Well, now that we are all experts on Vegemite, let me add that Vegemite, in addition to its other peculiar and interesting characteristics, has a very strong aroma. When the children opened the jar at breakfast, there was an audible gasp from the couple next to whom they were seated. These adorable children then proceeded to spread Vegemite over their entire breakfast—the grits, the sausage, the pound cake, the biscuits, the blueberry muffins—so that it looked as if someone had dropped a cup of brownish green paint on top of their plates. Rarely have I

45

seen the dining room clear out so quickly. I have to say, though, that those kids thoroughly enjoyed their breakfast!

One guest's breakfast preferences led us to make a permanent change in the way we serve breakfast. Most of our breakfast food offerings are presented on our side serving table so that guests can help themselves and so that we can easily refill things as they run out. One morning we had a gentlemen from Kentucky who was quite portly who came down to breakfast (Let's call him "Mr. Portly" for the time being). He told us he loved grits and sausage and was thrilled to see that was what was on the menu for the morning. As he made his way to the serving table, I saw him eying the sausage platter, a small porcelain platter on which two dozen link sausage were arranged in a neat pyramid, with silver tongs next to the platter so guests could help themselves. When Mr. Portly leaned over the platter, he exclaimed "Boy, these sure do look good!" and without bothering with the tongs, lifted the entire platter and deftly rolled all two dozen sausages onto his plate. My shock and consternation were matched or exceeded by that of the other guests, who hadn't yet gotten any sausage at all. Biting my tongue to hold back the various remarks about weight, health, manners, upbringing and so on that could have been made, I smiled, grabbed the platter, and went back to the kitchen, where I turned up the heat on the sausages in the skillet. In a few minutes, I made my way back to the dining room and with a flourish put the full, steaming platter back on the serving table with a mental "So there!" to the guest who had eaten the whole day's supply. Much to my dismay, Mr. Portly bounded up from his seat, and oblivious to the stunned silence of everyone else at the breakfast table, proceeded to empty the entire platter onto his plate again.

At least he solved one of my problems—I didn't have to worry whether I was burning the sausages left in the skillet while I was in the dining room, because we had now used up all the sausage we had in the house. And even though the other guests filing out of the dining room gave Mr. Portly cold, hostile, glances, I could be sure that there was at least ONE guest who had really enjoyed his breakfast.

In the spirit of continuous improvement and reengineering that was so much a part of corporate life in my previous career, we hit upon a brilliant solution so that this problem would never occur again: we now hold on to the sausage platter at all times. Whoever is serving breakfast will take the platter out to the dining room and graciously offer sausage to each seated guest, saying with a smile "Would you prefer one or two this morning?" They are not allowed to say "Would you like to test the health of your cardiovascular system by ingesting two dozen of these fat-filled lovelies at one sitting?" And the server is also instructed to hold on tight!

Besides all the excitement generated at breakfast by quirky food preferences, we also learned that sometimes what people wore to breakfast could be interesting as well. During the long, hot, humid summer days of July, it is surprising how many people choose Charleston as a wedding site. We attracted our fair share of newlyweds as guests, and it was always fun to see how they would arrive—by horse and carriage, by chauffeur-driven limousine, or even on foot. Our little girls especially enjoyed watching brides arrive who were still in their wedding gowns, which happened one night in July.

As we came home from having pizza, a bride and groom were arriving to check into Cypress, our big honeymoon suite with the king bed, jacuzzi, and romantic balcony. The bride had on a gorgeous ivory silk dress with lots of pearls and lace that the girls thought was just the most beautiful thing they had ever seen. You can imagine my surprise when next morning we saw the dress again at breakfast. At first we thought "Well, this girl is determined to get her money's worth out of this thing, and why not? It probably cost a fortune," until the groom took us aside to tell us that the bridesmaids, in a less-than-charming prank, had emptied all the bride's luggage, and all she had with her was literally the dress on her back!

A close brush with fame came this month as well, as we hosted some guests who told us they were being featured on *Good Morning America*, the nationally broadcast newscast. The hosts of the show were making a summer trek across the USA and broadcasting from a different state each day. In South Carolina, they decided to broadcast from Charleston's historic district in front of St. Michael's Church, just around the corner from our house. We had images in our mind of articulate, interesting guests mentioning to a national audience how much they loved Charleston and what a charming B&B they had found there, and imagined the wonderful flow of business that would result. We made sure their room had extra flowers and that everything was especially nice.

When the guests arrived, they turned out to be a mother and her two daughters, who let us know that the subject of the portion of the broadcast where they were to be featured was "unusual" pageants held in South Carolina and that both girls were beauty queens. One held the title of "Miss Chitlin'" and the other had recently been crowned "Miss Hell Hole Swamp." For those of you who don't know what a chitlin' is, the full spelling of the word is "chitterling." If that didn't help, don't worry—chitlins are definitely a specialty food and an acquired taste. They are fried hog intestines, and the town of Salley, South Carolina has a festival called the Salley Chitlin' Strut. I have always been afraid to inquire as to what the connection is between eating chitlins and strutting. Hell Hole Swamp is about 40 miles north of Charleston, and it too has a festival called (you guessed it) the Hell Hole Swamp Festival.

Both girls were lovely and asked for extra alarm clocks, as they had to be at the soundstage by 5 a.m. We wished them well and wondered what might happen if they mentioned our B&B on TV—what sort of guests night be attracted by the mention of chitlins and Hell Hole Swamp? Pushing visions of scenes from the movie *Deliverance* out of my mind, I retired for the evening but set my alarm so our whole family could go watch the show live.

When the girls appeared early the next morning, they were all decked out in iridescent spangled bathing suits and spike heels, wearing tiaras in their elaborately coiffed hair and banners proclaiming their titles. And they weren't alone—there were around 50 other beauty queens from competing festivals all arrayed for the television audience. Our two guests didn't get enough air time to mention where they were staying, which might have been a blessing in disguise, but they certainly did liven up breakfast when they walked into our dining room in their full regalia. All our other guests, especially the gentlemen, even paid close attention as the girls explained what a chitlin' was. You never know what you will learn when you stay at a B&B!

August

It was a beautiful early morning in Charleston, at least an hour before any guest would wake up and still cool before the raging heat of August days would kick in. As I looked around the recently renovated office of the bed and breakfast, I was delighted with the way things had turned out. Previously, when you walked in the lovely old front door of the house, with its delicate fanlight and early 19th century hardware and mellowed wooden floors, you looked straight across the entry foyer to a little back hall that featured right smack in the middle of your view a rusting 1960s hot water heater, with various pipes and a large metal vent to complete a picture that looked like some bad metal sculpture in a low-quality TriBeCa gallery. To add to this unfortunate picture, someone had in the same era installed two small windows near the hot water heater that were the squat kind you usually find in suburban ranch houses— they were about three feet tall and slightly oblong and aggressively ugly. We had decided to take this tiny space and make it into an office for the B&B, as it was conveniently located between the back door and the kitchen. It was easy to hear when guests were coming and going and to offer a word of greeting or ask if they needed help.

So, we had relocated and replaced the hot water heater and then had windows installed that matched the ones on the rest of the first floor of the house—wonderful tall windows that let in a flood of light—and the ones in the office were particularly pleasant, as they gave a view over the piazza and the courtyard garden with its camellias and tea olives and burbling fountain. Now, when you came in the front door, instead of focusing on an ugly hot water heater, you could see straight through to this tall window, with glimpses of the garden and kitchen house beyond, adding a tantalizing hint of new and charming discoveries to explore. It was a vast improvement.

We had painted the room a wonderful Chinese red, installed a black and white tile floor, and hung some blue, red, and yellow chintz curtains that picked up the colors in the Oriental rug, so now it was a very agreeable space, albeit a little small. As I pulled my chair up to the desk and looked out the window at the beams of sunlight on the old wicker rockers and swing on the piazza, I had to admit that things seemed to be turning out pretty well. The peaceful morning was a beautiful thing.

I opened up the calendar to check on the day's reservations and then pull the reservation forms for the guests arriving that day. We had developed these forms so we knew as much as possible about the guests coming in—special occasions they were celebrating, reservations we had made for them for tours or dinners or spa treatments, particular interests they wanted to explore, and so on. All this information was a huge help in trying to ensure that each guest's time in Charleston and at our B&B exceeded their expectations. When any of our staff took a reservation, the procedure was that they filled out the form completely, entered the last name and room assignment on the master calendar, and then completed a checklist to ensure everything would be done that the guests expected before their arrival.

As I looked at the reservation calendar, I noticed that there were two rooms of guests checking out that day and two rooms coming in, while the other four rooms had guests that would be staying through the end of the week. I leaned over to the standing file to pull the forms for the incoming guests to make sure everything was in order, and was surprised to find that there were three forms. I did a quick double-take and looked at the calendar again. As I did, a horrible sensation dawned upon me, as I realized that the unthinkable had happened—we had overbooked and had somehow given away a room that was supposed to be held for guests arriving that day.

Overbooking is an innkeeper's worst nightmare. Unlike airlines and hotels where overbooking is common, and can often be solved by shifting seats or flights or rearranging to a room on a different floor, bed and breakfasts like ours make reservations for particular rooms that have specific features, and when you have only six rooms, there is nowhere to rearrange people to. For people who have been planning their special get-away for months and months and have chosen your B&B above all the other lodging locations, getting bounced and being told "there is no room at the inn" is almost as bad as having your fiancée send you a "Dear John" letter with the ring enclosed.

"Yikes," I thought, "How could this happen?" Looking frantically through the paperwork, I saw that one of our staff had taken a reservation earlier that week from a booking agency, and that both parties were named Smith, and the staff person must have assumed that someone had already penciled in the guests' name from an earlier inquiry. It was an understandable mistake, but what was I going to tell the Smiths from Michigan when they arrived after a long flight and ready to check into their lovely and comfortable room? "Hit the road, Jack" did not seem to be a very considerate response, but I did not know what else we could do. As I glanced at their form, my heart sank—I remembered talking to these folks, and they were incredibly nice and had specifically decided to stay at our B&B after hearing about it from friends who had been some of our favorite guests so far. We had made lots of arrangements for them, and they were so excited to be coming to see us. I felt terrible, and knew they were going to be so disappointed.

What in the world were we going to do? There were lots of tourists in town coming for various special events in the historic district, and I highly doubted any of the comparable B&Bs or even hotels to whom we referred people when we were full would have any space.

As I was pondering and fretting about all this, our staff person arrived to get breakfast started, and my wife came downstairs for coffee, so I gathered them in the office for a quick pow-wow. We agreed it wasn't really fair to ask the Smiths who had checked in yesterday to move out in favor of the other Smiths coming in from Michigan, but that it would be worse than terrible to just tell the Michigan Smiths that they were on their own to try to find a place. Almost certainly, the four Smiths would not want to get cozy and all four stay in the same room with one king bed. We were going to have to get busy and find somewhere fabulous for the Michigan Smiths to stay, and I decided we would have to at least offer to pay for it ourselves—it was our fault, after all--and the last minute rate for somewhere nice was likely to be exorbitant.

This morning was not turning out at all the way I had imagined it, and now I realized with a further sinking heart that today was when I had promised to take the children on an excursion to the beach, and they were very excited about it. Now I knew that that was not going to happen, either, as I would be scurrying to try to resolve this overbooking problem. They were such sweet children, and we had been working with them on not complaining, so I knew they would pretend it was O.K., but I could see even now the quivering lips and the tears at the corners of their little eyes as the hoped-for excursion with Daddy got cancelled. Disappointment all around, and I was not seeing any good options.

As soon as breakfast was over and the guests sent on their way, I sat down with the children and explained what had happened and that we were not going to be able to go to the beach after all. They listened quietly, slumping a bit sadly as I broke the news, and I did see the hint of some tears. Fortunately, Whit, the oldest, had a great suggestion—maybe they could put on their new bathing suits and use the new sprinkler and water toys we had bought and have a water play-day in the side garden, which had recently been sodded and now had a luxuriant crop of thick green grass. I said I thought that sounded like a great idea, and I asked him if he would be willing to keep an eye on his two younger sisters. He gave me a big smile and said "Yes sir—you can count on me!"

Well, at least that was one crisis that looked on its way to a happy ending, so I proceeded to try to find a room for the Michigan Smiths. I called place after place, spending long periods of time on hold, as I wanted to speak to the owner of each establishment to see if there was anything they could possibly do to help. I got a lot of sympathy, but everywhere I called was completely booked up. I then started in on upscale hotels in the historic district, and everywhere I called it was the same story— they were so sorry, they understood completely the terrible predicament we were in, they had had similar experiences themselves and wished they could help, but they just did not have a room to spare at any price. After over three hours on the phone, all to no avail, I was starting to feel not only upset but increasingly desperate. I put my head down on the office desk and began to pray.

"O Lord, please help me find a room for these folks. Please, please. I don't know what to do."

I felt a little hand patting my shoulder and looked up to see Mary Hollis, my four-year-old, standing by me and saying "It will be OK, Daddy, don't cry."

How I wished I could believe her…

Looking up at the clock, I realized that it was only 30 minutes before the Michigan Smiths would be arriving at the front door. It was tempting to leave and have my staff deal with the awkward and possibly hostile situation of telling them that not only did we not have a room for them, but no one else did either and they might have to drive to Myrtle Beach to find a room, and then probably at a motel full of motorcyclists. I realized, though, that was the coward's way out; I would just have to tell them the truth and beg for mercy.

I decided to get up from the desk for a minute and go sit out on the swing to see if it would lighten my mood and the weight of the world that seemed to be resting between my shoulders. As I sat there, I could hear the sounds of the children playing in the sprinkler. They had on their new matching bathing suits and the three of them looked adorable, jumping in and out of the sprinkler and playing with their little water guns. They seemed to have gotten over the loss of their beach day, and Whit was doing a great job of keeping them entertained. I was beginning to feel a little better, when suddenly the back door flew open and my wife ran out toward me waving her hands over her head and shouting "Thank God, thank God—your friend Paul just called and they had a last-minute cancellation on a suite for exactly the right number of nights. He said to call him right back if you want it."

Well, that was the best news I had heard in a long time! I flew into the office and called Paul's personal number, and sure enough, he had a wonderful suite that was open for just the right number of nights that also had the king bed the guests had requested. I thanked him profusely and said of course we would take it right away and pay for it ourselves. I explained to him what delightful people the Smiths had been all through the reservations process and told him I would count it as a great personal favor if he would give them as much personal attention as he could. He said they would do their best for us.

What a Godsend! Paul's B&B was one of my favorite establishments in Charleston, in a great location and run by good folks who were from Charleston. I hoped the Smiths might like it and it might ease their disappointment a little. I began to feel like I could breathe again.

Right then the doorbell rang, and I went to the door. An attractive middle aged couple was there on the front steps with a good bit of expensive-looking luggage. I opened the door, and before I could say a word they both broke into big smiles and the wife said "Hello! We are the Smiths from Michigan, and we are so thrilled to be here! Driving down the street in the taxi, I thought it was even more beautiful than we had imagined it could be, and your location is just fabulous. And our taxi driver knew about your place and told us it was one of the very best places in town to stay. We cannot wait to get into that beautiful room you were so kind to send us pictures of, and to spend some time with you and hear about what you think would be the best way to spend our time in Charleston. This is going to be a dream vacation for us both, all thanks to you!"

Well, at this point, I was equally torn between collapsing in tears at their feet while beating my breast and chanting "mea culpa, mea culpa, mea maxima culpa," or running screaming down the street as far away from the B&B as I could get. I mustered a trembling smile and invited them in, thanking them for their kind words.

"Come on into the Drawing Room. Could I bring you some lemonade or some iced tea?"

"Lemonade would be great, thank you. What a gorgeous room. And is this all your family furniture? It is just beautiful."

I ducked into the kitchen and asked our staffperson to bring out some lemonade and benne wafers. In the Gullah tradition, benne wafers are supposed to bring good luck, and I needed all the help I could get.

Going back to the Drawing Room in a few minutes, I saw the Smiths with their lemonade and benne wafers looking supremely happy. I had a feeling that expression was getting ready to change. I figured I'd better jump right in before things got any worse.

"I am so delighted to get to meet you both, and I am so sorry to say I have some bad news. I am afraid that our staff made a mistake and accidentally doublebooked the room you had reserved. The other guests had the same last name, and so the mistake did not get caught until this morning. I take full responsibility for this, and I do apologize from the bottom of my heart."

The wife, looking crestfallen, said "Do you mean we can't stay here? Oh no! You don't have any room where you could put us? Part of the reason we came to Charleston was to stay with you especially, and now the whole experience will not be at all what we had been planning. I have been looking forward to this for months. Oh my, oh my, oh my."

"I am so deeply sorry," I said. "The good news is that I did call around and found you a wonderful suite at one of our other favorite B&Bs in Charleston. I would be happy to drive you over—it's just a few blocks—and you can look at it to see whether you think it would suit. I will insist on paying for it because it was our mistake."

The husband patted his wife on the back, saying "Honey, I am really sad about this, too. We put so much work into choosing a special place for our get-away, and it is hard not to be extremely disappointed. But it sounds like we don't have much choice. I guess we should go look at the other place. And it's nice of you to offer to pay, but we may just decide to go home. This is all very disappointing."

I helped them with their luggage and we headed out the back door to walk through the courtyard to the side street where my car was parked. The Smiths perked up a little bit when they saw the children. "Oh, what darling children—and look at those cute matching bathing suits! What a wonderful experience for them to grow up in such a beautiful place!"

"Children, can you come say hello to the Smiths?"

The children turned from the sprinkler and headed over in our direction to say hello. I do have to say they looked pretty cute, with their hair glowing in the sun and their tans set off against their colorful swimsuits and their playful banter with each other. When they got about four feet from us, Mary Hollis, the four-year-old, looked up at us with a big smile on her face. Stopping and gazing up at the Smiths, she giggled and squeezed tight on the trigger of her enormous water gun, shooting a huge jet of extremely cold water right straight into Mr. Smith's crotch, soaking him thoroughly.

"Take me now, Lord," I prayed. "Please, Lord, right this second!"

Well, I was still here, so I figured I'd better start

trying to deal with an already awkward situation which had just gotten immeasurably worse. I mean, here we were, throwing these nice people out after their long morning of travel, people who had wanted to stay with us more than anything, people who had not yelled or screamed at me (yet), people who were the kind of guests we really enjoyed having—and now our sweet little girl had soaked this poor man's pants in the worst possible place.

As I began to fumble for words to apologize, Mr. Smith proved his true character by looking at Mary Hollis and her water gun and his pants and then beginning to laugh with great gusto. Before long, his wife started laughing too, and the children (somewhat nervously) began giggling. I still wasn't feeling it, but did manage a smile.

Mr. Smith leaned over, patted me on the back, and said "I can tell you are not having a great day. Don't worry about my pants; I am sure they will dry, and someday you will look back on this and laugh. Let's go check out this other place."

Well, I never really knew if perhaps the Smiths were secretly glad to have escaped to another bed and breakfast where they did not have to worry about any scenarios like *Lord of the Flies* where perhaps the children would move on from assault by water gun to something more serious, but when we got to Paul's place, they professed to love it. I helped them get settled in and drove back over in a few minutes with all the directions to their various dinners and tours starting from where they were now staying, plus a flower arrangement and a bottle of wine to thank them for being so nice about it.

I checked with them each day of their four-day stay, and they raved about Paul and their suite and how much they were enjoying all the places we had suggested. They very politely avoided mentioning that we had let them down through this whole overbooking fiasco. On the day they checked out, Paul called and said the Smiths had absolutely insisted on paying for their suite and not allowing us to pick up the tab, and had told him to let us know how much they appreciated everything. I resolved to write them a note in a few days to thank them for being so gracious after we had disappointed them, and breathed a sigh of relief that the whole thing had ended without fisticuffs or lawsuits.

Two days later, a FedEx package arrived for me. I opened it, and was surprised to find a whole array of toys and gadgets for the children and some little gifts for the B&B. Included with the package was a note—from Mr. Smith! Imagine my surprise as I read it and discovered that they had sent me a thank you note for bouncing them so nicely. They said they had never been treated so well, and that because we had (to their way of thinking), gone so far above and beyond the call of duty in making sure that they still had a great vacation, they could not wait until they could come back and stay with us and continue their exploration of Charleston. Mr. Smith even said to make sure to say hello to the darling little girl with the water gun.

They might have been from Michigan, but the Smiths were the perfect example of what we mean in the South when we say "That man is good people."

September

September in Charleston is perhaps the least charming month of the year but arguably one of the most exciting. While other parts of the country are starting to experience the cool, crisp air of autumn, down here the hot, humid weather that sits on the city like a wet blanket means that outdoor activity becomes a challenge--unless you don't mind looking like a drowned rat as you become soaked from perspiration. In Charleston, even the windows sweat in September. Since the dewpoint can be in the mid-70s on high humidity days, we would often wake in the morning and be unable to see out the windows because of all the condensation resulting from the warm, humid air hitting our air-conditioned windows.

September is also the month that the mildew

rampage begins in earnest—anything that is damp which is left outdoors for more than a few hours will soon be covered with small black spots that are the beginnings of mildew. Boards on our house that have begun to rot will sprout mushrooms during September. But chief among September delights is the prospect of a hurricane hitting the city- tearing your roof off, blowing out your windows, and filling your house with five feet (or more) of slime that includes black, oozy pluff mud and the dank remains of marine creatures.

The delicate beauty of Charleston's architecture, with its fine attention to detail, seems oddly out of place with climatic realities. In a region with humidity, salt air, and the risk of high winds and enormous storm surges like tsunamis from hurricanes, it seems the height of folly to build ornate wooden houses, not to mention beautiful gardens where one blast of a salt water wave will poison the earth for years to come. But, Charlestonians have never been known to have logic as their strong suit. Perhaps it is better to think of the persistence of Charleston not as the height of folly, akin to the Biblical character who builds his house upon the sand, but as a courageous challenge to the elements, and the indomitable will to outlast and rebuild no matter what cataclysmic event may occur.

In these days of doppler radar, hurricane hunting aircraft, and computer-generated storm tracks with attendant strike probability charts, we are now treated to weeks of speculation each time a storm appears in the tropics as to whether it might hit us, and worst of all whether it may follow the same track as Hugo, the infamous 1989 hurricane that did not turn to the north as polite hurricanes are supposed to do as they approach Charleston, but instead barreled down on the city and vented its furor on the Lowcountry landscape. The local television news shows are full of this each evening during hurricane season. The problem is, of course, that no one REALLY has any idea of where the storm may go. In some ways, people in the 18th century had an easier time of it. If the clouds turned really black and the wind kicked up, they knew they were in for something and would close up their shutters and bide their time, hoping and praying to avoid destruction. They were blissfully unaware of all of those other storms that were out there but turned and went elsewhere, so that their lives were not focused on storms for weeks or months at a time.

Hurricane prediction models have improved somewhat, so that now you can usually expect 24 hours notice before a storm hits you, which for most normal people gives them adequate time to do last-minute preparations and evacuate.

Alas, I fear we do not fall into the category of normal people. Our first problem is our house, which is definitely not normal, even for an historic Charleston home. One thing that we love about the house is that it gets great light, as many of the rooms have windows on all three sides. Of course, when you are battening down the hatches for a hurricane, the first thing you are supposed to do is to board up all the windows so that the high winds do not hurl projectiles that smash the windows and then let in the elements. This month, when we had our first real hurricane scare, we went outside to count the windows and to imagine how long it would take to secure them. After a few tries, we concluded that it would take about an hour per window to secure them properly, which included the time to drag out the enormous ladder required for the job. The problem is that when we counted, we learned that we had 79 windows. If we did one window per hour and worked round the clock for 24 hours without breaks for food or rest, we would need at least 3.5 days' notice to get the house ready, which reveals another problem: the landfall point for a hurricane that is still three or more days away can vary over an area of hundreds of miles. So, you can be like Noah and begin building the ark while no one believes there will be a storm and endure the ridicule and the lost labor and lost money you spent on supplies for boarding up, or you can take your chances and only do as many windows as you have time for once it is clear that the storm is really coming after you.

Another aspect in which we are not normal is in having lots of irreplaceable antique family furniture—perhaps not especially valuable to anyone else, but redolent of memories of beloved relatives. Some people in Charleston take the attitude of *que sera, sera* with hurricanes, reasoning that if they are well-insured they can rebuild and refurnish, perhaps even to a higher standard than before the storm. This attitude is no comfort if you have family things that you want to protect. Since we are only twelve houses away from Charleston harbor, our whole first floor in the main house and both floors of the kitchen house (which is built on the grade) are at risk from a storm surge during a hurricane, which means that everything on those floors has to be moved upstairs. Naturally, the drawing room and dining room have the biggest, heaviest furniture in the whole house—mahogany linen presses, early Empire sofas, a grand piano, big Oriental rugs, and so on—and the furniture on the second floor of the kitchen house can come out only by taking the balcony apart, pulling a pick-up truck into the driveway below it, and doing a three-part removal process where furniture goes out on the balcony, is then handed down to the truck, and is then handed down to someone on the ground, who can then hand the furniture down to the person waiting on the ground who gets to carry it across the garden and thence upstairs in the main house, meanwhile not smashing anything in the

70

process.

Yet another factor that further complicates our storm preparation activity schedule is the fact that we have a B&B which attracts guests from all over the world, many of whom are totally clueless about hurricanes. It is one of the most delicate aspects of being an innkeeper to walk the fine line between two alternatives: (1) assuring your guests that everything is fine and that the storm is going to turn and go somewhere else so that they do not panic and flee, leaving you with empty rooms and no income, or (2) inducing panic by telling them what a storm can do, that the airport will likely close, that they need to find an alternative way out of the area, and that if there is a mandatory evacuation order, we will all be forced to leave—and then smiling nicely and asking if they know how to swim.

The Saffir-Simpson scale of hurricane intensity divides hurricanes into categories based on potential for destructions, and while the scale is well-known to residents of coastal areas, it sounds like arcane jeweler's lingo to the uninitiated.

The Saffir-Simpson Hurricane Scale
The Saffir-Simpson Hurricane Scale is a 1-5 rating based on the hurricane's present intensity. This is used to give an estimate of the potential property damage and flooding expected along the coast from a hurricane landfall. Wind speed is the determining factor in the scale, as storm surge values are highly dependent on the slope of the continental shelf in the landfall region. Note that all winds are using the U.S. 1-minute average.

Category One Hurricane: Winds 74-95 mph (64-82 kt--119-153 km/hr). Storm surge generally 4-5 ft above normal. No real damage to building structures. Damage primarily to unanchored mobile homes, shrubbery, and trees. Some damage to poorly constructed signs. Also, some coastal road flooding and minor pier damage. Hurricanes Allison of 1995 and Danny of 1997 were Category One hurricanes at peak intensity.

Category Two Hurricane: Winds 96-110 mph (83-95 kt--154-177 km/hr). Storm surge generally 6-8 feet above normal. Some roofing material, door, and window damage of buildings. Considerable damage to shrubbery and trees with some trees blown down. Considerable damage to mobile homes, poorly constructed signs, and piers. Coastal and low-lying escape routes flood 2-4 hours before arrival of the hurricane center. Small craft in unprotected anchorages break moorings. Hurricane Bonnie of 1998 was a Category Two hurricane when it hit the North Carolina coast, while Hurricane Georges of 1998 was a Category Two Hurricane when it hit the Florida Keys and Mississippi.

Category Three Hurricane: Winds 111-130 mph (96-113 kt or 178-209 km/hr). Storm surge generally 9-12 ft above normal. Some structural damage to small residences and utility buildings with a minor amount of curtainwall failures. Damage to shrubbery and trees with foliage blown off trees and large trees blown down. Mobile homes and poorly constructed signs are destroyed. Low-lying escape routes are cut by rising water 3-5 hours before arrival of the center of the hurricane. Flooding near the coast destroys smaller structures with larger structures damaged by battering from floating debris. Terrain continuously lower than 5 ft above mean sea level may be flooded inland 8 miles (13 km) or more. Evacuation of low-lying residences with several blocks of the shoreline may be required. Hurricanes Roxanne of 1995 and Fran of 1996 were Category Three hurricanes at landfall on the Yucatan Peninsula of Mexico and in North Carolina, respectively.

Category Four Hurricane: Winds 131-155 mph (114-135 kt or 210-249 km/hr). Storm surge generally 13-18 ft above normal. More extensive curtainwall failures with some complete roof structure failures on small residences. Shrubs, trees, and all signs are blown down. Complete destruction of mobile homes. Extensive damage to doors and windows. Low-lying escape routes may be cut by rising water 3-5 hours before arrival of the center of the hurricane. Major damage to lower floors of structures near the shore. Terrain lower than 10 ft above sea level may be flooded requiring massive evacuation of residential areas as far inland as 6 miles (10 km). Hurricane Luis of 1995 was a Category Four hurricane while moving over the Leeward Islands. Hurricanes Felix and Opal of 1995 also reached Category Four status at peak intensity.

Category Five Hurricane: Winds greater than 155 mph (135 kt or 249 km/hr). Storm surge generally greater than 18 ft above normal. Complete roof failure on many residences and industrial buildings. Some complete building failures with small utility buildings blown over or away. All shrubs, trees, and signs blown down. Complete destruction of mobile homes. Severe and extensive window and door damage. Low-lying escape routes are cut by rising water 3-5 hours before arrival of the center of the hurricane. Major damage to lower floors of all structures located less than 15 ft above sea level and within 500 yards of the shoreline. Massive evacuation of residential areas on low ground within 5-10 miles (8-16 km) of the shoreline may be required. Hurricane Mitch of 1998 was a Category Five hurricane at peak intensity over the western Caribbean. Hurricane Gilbert of 1988 was a Category Five hurricane at peak intensity and is one of the strongest Atlantic tropical cyclones of record. – *National Hurricane Center*

Once you've lived in Charleston for a while, you realize that tropical storms and Category One hurricanes are not really a big deal, especially if they do not hit at high tide and if you live in a part of town not prone to flooding. We were fortunate, as our street is the spine of the

Charleston peninsula and rarely floods. However, if you get a hurricane that is a Category Two, you are going to have to do some prep work on your house to protect it. With a Category Three, you will do lots of prep work and then leave town. With Category Four and Five, you will do what you can to prepare, book it out of town as fast as you can., and pray that there will be something left that you recognize when you return after the storm.

I had been watching with a wary eye a storm that had been forming down off the coast of Florida. Right now, the weather was beautiful—bright blue skies, reasonable humidity, and we were sold out on all of our rooms through the weekend as guests enjoyed boat tours and outings to the beach. There were storms forming all summer long every year that left us alone, but for some reason I had a bad feeling about this one. I continued to watch as the storm grew, and now forecasters were saying it could be a Category 4 or even Category 5 monster when it made landfall. Although most of our guests loved our "lose touch with the world--no television, no WiFi, immerse yourself in Charleston" experience, I did feel obliged to let them know that there was a storm out there we were watching. So long as the sky is blue, though, it is hard to convince people that there might be a problem, and most of them shrugged it off. I did remind them that if they had flown in, they should check with their airlines about flight arrangements and the storm's potential effect on them.

There was no need to panic, though—not yet, anyway. I did call my sister in Atlanta to see if they were worried about their beach house in Charleston, and she said they were keeping an eye on the storm and if it looked bad they were going to come over to try to secure their place. I said I would be glad to help, but she said if the storm came she knew our hands would be full and she was sure they could manage.

When I came down to the office the next morning, I saw on the computer that the storm had grown even stronger and that they were ordering an evacuation of the entire east coast of Florida. Although they did not expect the storm to make landfall in Florida, it was such a huge hurricane and so strong that the edge passing over Florida would bring Category 3 winds and storm surges, enough to do serious damage. I thought that sounded pretty bad and decided to log on to the National Hurricane Center's website. If the storm wasn't going to make landfall in Florida, I wondered where they thought it was going. Hoping to see a storm track that took the monster back out to sea, or maybe up to a sparsely populated area of the Outer Banks, I was shocked to see that the new forecast track they had just released indicated that the center of the hurricane would make landfall at Edisto Beach, South

Carolina, as a Category 4 or 5 storm in approximately 36 hours.

If you live in downtown Charleston, that forecast is enough to strike terror into your heart. Edisto Beach is about 30 miles south of Charleston, and the worst place you can be in a hurricane is on the north side of the center, as that is where the strongest storm surge comes, hurtling massive waves and winds at your house.

Just as I was reading this, I heard a knock on the front door, and went out to find an officer from one of the local emergency preparedness offices. He said he was trying to get the word out to all the lodging establishments that this was potentially a catastrophic storm; he then pointed to the front wall of our house, saying "See those tall windows you have there on the first floor? Our models are predicting you will have storm surge water to the top of those windows if this thing hits Edisto at high tide, and that could be as soon as 36 hours from now. You had better get your people out of here—there is going to be a mandatory evacuation order coming soon."

Well, that is the kind of knock on the door that can ruin your morning. As I walked back in the house in a state of shock, I saw that most of our guests were in the dining room enjoying a convivial breakfast and chatting about plans for the day and who was going where for dinner that night. I couldn't face going in there and telling them what was about to happen, and I also wanted to make sure what I had just heard was correct. I went back to the office and checked the National Weather Service site for Charleston, as well as the Emergency Management website for Charleston County. Sure enough, a mandatory evacuation order had just been issued for the South Carolina coast east of Highway 17, with people being told to leave before noon today. Meanwhile, the phone was ringing off the hook with people from Florida who had been forced to evacuate who thought Charleston would be safe, but we had to tell them that the storm was now heading this way and they had better start praying and try to head inland. The news reports were now predicting what sounded like Armageddon when the storm made landfall, and also commented that we were now in the midst of the largest peacetime evacuation in U.S. history.

As soon as I heard that, my very first call was to my contact at the downtown Enterprise Rent-A-Car office with whom we did a lot of business. I gave him my credit card and said to hold four cars, I didn't care what they were, for me for an hour and on no account to rent them to someone else until he heard back from me. I knew four rooms of our guests had flown in, and I was pretty confident that none of them had made arrangements to get out of the city, and I was sure that their flights were going to be cancelled.

As I walked into the dining room, all the guests were there, and it was a beautiful sight—bountiful fresh flowers, the crystal chandelier sparkling, delicious food on the table, the silver flatware and serving pieces and the Waterford crystal all shining in the sun coming in through the windows, attractive and interesting guests from around the country savoring some time to unwind in a lovely place. And I was about to give them news that would be not unlike yelling "FIRE! FIRE!" in a crowded theater. I cleared my throat loudly and as they turned to me, smiling expectantly, I said "Ladies and gentlemen, I am afraid I have some bad news. The storm I have been mentioning for the past few days has become a major hurricane, one of the three strongest since they have been keeping records, and it is headed our way, so we are going to have to make preparations."

A woman from Vancouver interrupted me, "Oh, I am sure we will be fine. You have all those nice umbrellas out there, and we won't mind a little rain—we're used to that at home." She turned back to her friends and started chattering and everyone started to settle back into their repasts.

At this point, I had a vivid image randomly pop into my head of an episode from the old British comedy "Fawlty Towers" which John Cleese of Monty Python fame wrote, directed, and starred in as Basil Fawlty, the

77

innkeeper. It was set in a coastal B&B in England and hilariously chronicled the challenges and joys of running a B&B. It was good therapy, too, because often he and his staff told off difficult guests in ways that we might have been tempted to emulate, but never dared. In the episode that had popped into my mind, the staff had been testing the fire alarm and did a fire drill with the guests, only to have a real fire break out a few hours later. Basil was terrified and tried to convince his guests of their impending danger, but no one would pay him any mind. I was feeling a bit like Basil, starting to panic, and now my mind flashed to the Titanic and the orchestra playing as the officers assured everyone that things were perfectly fine, while in fact the mortally wounded ship was sinking. Clearly, I needed to get a grip and get their attention.

Clearing my throat loudly again, I said in a very emphatic voice, "Ladies and gentlemen, I am afraid this is not just a matter of a little rain, but potentially a catastrophic natural disaster that may be life-threatening." Well, that had got their attention. You could have heard a pin drop now. I continued, "In fact, we have just gotten word that the Governor of South Carolina has ordered a mandatory evacuation of the entire coast of South Carolina east of Highway 17, including downtown Charleston, and everyone is required to leave by noon today."

At this point, there was a commotion at the table as

a woman from Manhattan fell out of her chair as she jumped to her feet waving her hands and screaming "Oh my God! Oh my God! We are ALL going to DIE!! Oh my God!" There was mixture of shock, awe, and terror on the faces of the other guests, and I jumped back into the fray, outshouting the woman and saying "MADAM, MADAM, please CONTROL yourself!! No one is going to die, at least not if you pay attention to me. Now everyone needs to listen very carefully."

"Those of you who flew in, remember I spoke with you two days ago about having a contingency transportation plan like a rental car in case the storm came this way. Did any of you make plans?"

There was utter silence, some sheepish looks, and finally one gentleman said "The weather has been so beautiful, it just didn't seem possible we would need any arrangements."

His wife turned on him, snarling, "WHAT! You mean you knew this might happen and you didn't DO ANYTHING? Are you CRAZY? You mean we are stuck here to DIE? Oh my God!" and then she dissolved into sobs.

I jumped in again, "PLEASE do not panic. Listen to me. I have four rental cars on hold at Enterprise that you can reserve, but we need to get them pronto, as there are going to be hundreds if not thousands of people trying to get these cars—they may be the last ones available."

Another guest from Wyoming, who clearly knew nothing about hurricanes, jumped in. "Can't we just stay here? I mean, this house is nearly 300 years old and it must have made it through a lot of storms. We can just fill up the bathtubs for drinking water. It might be kind of exciting!"

I looked him in the eye and said in a very calm voice, "Sir, the area where you are sitting right now, the stairs, and indeed this entire room right up to the chandelier are likely to be full of ocean water and marine life within 36 hours. And the evacuation is MANDATORY. Staying here is not an option."

I should have known that the ocean water and marine life would be too much for the woman from New York, who began screaming and crying again "I knew it! We are all going to DIE! If we don't drown, now we will probably be eaten by SHARKS just like in "JAWS"! Oh my GOD-what are we going to do?"

I jumped in again, "Ladies and gentlemen, there is no need to panic. What you need to do is to pack immediately and check out—we will, of course, waive any cancellation fees for the remaining nights of your reservation, and those of you who have your cars need to get on the road right away to get out of town—the traffic is going to be horrendous."

"The rest of you need to leave one person here to pack and check out and send the other person with me to go get the rental cars in ten minutes. We will meet by the back door in ten minutes and I will drive you to the rental car office in our van. I know this is a scary and unfamiliar situation, but I promise if you do not panic and you do what I just said, everything will be fine."

Having said all this with a smile and a calm confidence that I did not really feel, I said "Let's get to it!" and they all leapt up from the table and headed for their rooms.

Now that I had dealt with their panic, I had to figure out how to deal with my own. We had four hours before we were supposed to evacuate, and I needed to get our family packed up and figure out where we were going to go, board up the house, move all the furniture from the first floor up to the second floor, and move all the furniture out of the kitchen house (since it was built right on ground level and had lower ceilings, both floors were likely to be underwater in a ten foot storm surge). I needed to get the guests out of here as soon as possible, not only for their own safety, but so we could secure the house. I needed to try to express a sense of urgency to my wife and children, while not inciting panic, especially since my wife was 8 months pregnant and the low barometric pressure that comes with hurricanes often induces early labor.

That was more than I could think about at this point, so I refused to let my mind even consider what it would be like to try to deliver a baby single-handed in the midst of all this chaos. I had eight minutes before I had to drive the guests up to Enterprise, and like the desperate man in jail who can only make one phone call, I knew who I needed--Michael Gregg, our painter friend. I called his cell number and anxiously prayed he would pick up. Sure enough, on the second ring he did:

"Well, hello there, Mr. Brian-I thought I might be hearing from you. I have my men downtown and we can come on over and get your windows boarded up if you like."

"Michael, you are an answer to prayer. Please come and I will pay you anything within reason if you can help me out."

"No problem, Mr. Brian. We will be right there."

And then it hit me. We had no wood--what was he going to use to board up the windows? The lines at Lowe's and Home Depot would be unimaginable now, and they probably did not have enough wood supplies anyway. As I was having mental images of our lovely early 19th century windows with their original glass blown out and lying in shards across the garden because we had not thought to get supplies in advance to board them up, I looked out the office window and beheld a beautiful sight that I thought must be a mirage—there were my sister and nephew pulling up with the top of her van covered with a huge stack of lumber. I went bounding out of the house to greet her with a big hug, and she said, "I was watching the news and saw how bad it was going to be here, and I figured you wouldn't be able to find wood to board the house up, so we decided to bring you some. Could you use it?"

I started to cry and gave her another hug. "You just have no idea. You are an answer to prayer. We had nothing, and I didn't know what we were going to do. Thank you SO much—but I know you need to hurry and get out of here so you can get to work on your beach house."

"Well, no--we actually drove all night and got here about 4 am and have already taken care of our place at the beach, so what can we do to help you out here?"

This was too good to be true. My sister, who is an organizational genius and beloved aunt whom our children adore, and my strong, athletic 18-year-old nephew, were indeed an answer to prayer. I said "I have got to take these guests to pick up rental cars so they can evacuate. If you can get the children fed and organized and packed, and if you can get your son to start moving furniture up to the second floor of the main house, that would be unbelievably helpful."

"No problem," she said. "We will get right on it."

83

I got the guests into the van and hurried up to Enterprise, where everything was in perfect order, and they followed my van back to the B&B in a little parade of rental cars. We got their luggage loaded up, and they thanked us for a great stay, hugging us and wishing us luck before hotfooting it down the road.

Now that the guests were gone, Michael Gregg and his crew and my nephew got to work, and four hours later the windows were all secured, save one at the very top of the third floor that we could not reach with the ladder, and the bulk of the furniture had been moved upstairs. We were an hour past the mandatory evacuation deadline, but everyone had done yeoman's work. My sister had all the children packed up with their favorite stuffed animals, and we had another small parade, driving out of a deserted city in our vans, as we drove to the fourth level of a nearby parking deck to put our other car out of the reach of floodwaters. How we hoped there would be something to come back to after the storm!

October

It took us 15 hours to get to Georgia, where we were evacuating to my parents' house, a trip that normally took five or six hours, but this time was complicated by a boneheaded decision by the Governor to not reverse all the lanes of the interstate highway going out of Charleston to facilitate traffic flow. It took us three hours just to get from downtown Charleston to the airport exit, which is usually a twenty-minute drive. Fifteen hours with three small children and a very pregnant wife, and the stress of imagining that your new B&B, into which you have poured your heart and soul, not to mention all your worldly possessions, might be leveled by a killer storm --and there was not one thing you could do about it.

Fortunately for us, the storm veered away from Charleston at the last moment, and weakened significantly, and evacuees were soon given clearance to return home.

Driving back into town, there was debris everywhere and most places still had no power, but it did not look too bad. We held our breath as we made our way slowly down our street, stopping from time to time to move big limbs out of the way. When we pulled up in front of our house, we breathed an enormous sigh of relief—it was still there, and looked to be in great shape. There were limbs and debris all around, but the boards over the windows were all still in place. We ran through the house doing a quick assessment of damage, and the only real problem was on the third floor, where the one window we had not boarded up had blown out completely, so there was some broken glass and water damage, but otherwise the main house was unscathed. The kitchen house was in great shape, too— Michael Gregg's crew had done a fine job and all the boards had held there as well.

The only odd thing we found was a beautiful Golden Retriever who was sleeping on our piazza and seemed affectionately determined to follow us everywhere we went. The children were thrilled, and of course wanted to keep the dog, but as we looked at the tags, we saw he belonged to a neighbor down the street. We sent the children to take him home, and the owners' cries of delight at being reunited with their furry friend helped mollify the children's sadness at not keeping a new pet.

As we got to work at cleaning everything up and re-opening the house, we were reminded again that this was too much for two adults to manage. One thing we had learned quickly after opening the B&B was that it was imperative to have some outside help, as managing our children and all the daily tasks of the B&B while simultaneously being gracious to guests and appearing to be unhurried and at leisure for chats with them at any moment was a challenge, to say the least. Part of the B&B experience is the mystique of an oasis of calm and graciousness (*calme, luxe, et volupt*é, as the French put it), even though you as the owner may be dealing with backed-up toilets, recalcitrant roofers, or wasp infestations. In fact, one of the books we had read before opening the B&B suggested that one way to preserve this mystique for guests was to always make a point during telephone conversations with potential guests to say "Could you excuse me just a moment? I have to take the muffins out of the oven. I'll be right back." Well, there were never going to be any muffins in our oven if we didn't get busy, as all our help was going back to college for the fall term, and we were going to be on our own.

Fortunately, Charleston is a college town with literally tens of thousands of college students. The nearest college to us was the College of Charleston, founded in 1770 and more importantly within walking or biking distance of our B&B. I decided to go up to the placement office at the College and put up a posting on their part-time jobs board. Surely students who were coming to a college that prided itself on its ancient heritage and its well-preserved campus located right in the heart of the historic district would jump at the chance to work in an historic B&B. I set to work writing the job posting, emphasizing professional appearance and the importance of submitting a resume in order to obtain an interview. Now all I would have to do is sort through the stacks of resumes that would come our way and then select which ones to interview.

As I walked home from the college placement office along King Street, I was reminded again of the street's intense vitality, so different from the slow pace and occasional empty and often dilapidated storefronts I remembered as a boy. Though I missed the wonderful service and beautiful courtyard at Jack Krawcheck's and though it was hard to reconcile the creaky old escalators inside Kerrison's with the huge posters of half-naked people hanging in the space now that it had become Abercrombie & Fitch, it was hard to argue that as a whole the street was greatly improved, even if there was no longer an Olde Colony Bakeshop to stop into for a cookie.

I had scarcely been home for an hour when the doorbell rang and our afternoon assistant let me know that someone was there wanting to talk to me about the job opening. I was very surprised since the job had just been posted, and a little annoyed since I had specifically asked for resumes rather than drop-ins, but I thought that the eagerness and effort of coming straight over to apply might be a sign of a superior candidate, so I went out to the Drawing Room to invite the candidate back to the office.

Entering the door, I was nearly struck dumb (a very rare condition for a B&B owner, who has to have a ready stream of conversation at all times) as a I gazed at the applicant. She was nearly six feet tall, with jet black hair piled up on her head in a series of combs. She was wearing a floor-length black gown with a gauzy skirt that fell in pennant scarf-like pleats to the ground and a very tight strapless bodice encasing her avoirdupois and displaying a good bit of cleavage. Around her shoulders and neck was a black gauze cape with glitter woven into it. She had on so much make-up she could easily have been getting ready to go onstage for "La Traviata," except that disconcertingly this make-up carried on the glitter theme, so that she was sparkling from her cleavage right on up to her scalp. Her stiletto heels were probably already wreaking havoc on our 19th century floors, and her black lipstick, black nailpolish, and black toenail polish (complete with embedded rhinestones on each nail) combined with her heavy mascara to create a ghoulish look,

My first thought was that they were holding auditions for Elvira, Lady of the Night, and she had gotten the wrong address, but as I entered the room she turned to me, hand outstretched and said "I'm Faye Marie and I want to interview for the B&B job." Her deep country Southern accent was at odds with her vampirish appearance, and I was so flustered that I just motioned for her to follow me, afraid to even try to say anything for fear that all I might be able to get out would be a yelp of horror, as I had visions of her opening the door to greet guests and having them run screaming in the other direction, thinking they had met the Bride of Frankenstein.

As she settled her ample self onto the chair in the office, she adjusted her bodice and scarf to display her charms in what she must have thought was the most alluring fashion and said "I would just love to work in a B&B. I love to get all dressed up like this so that I fit right in with history. This is a classy kind of place, I can tell, and I like nice things."

I resisted the urge to tell her that the kind of history where she would fit in would more likely be found in Transylvania rather than Charleston, and instead nudged her back toward the front door, telling her that we would be in touch.

After ushering her out the door, I was speculating on what was missing in our job posting about professional appearance and sending a resume—perhaps I should have added a section in bold and highlighted in bright neon yellow marker that said "THIS IS **REALLY** IMPORTANT IF YOU WANT THIS JOB!" As I pondered this, the doorbell rang again, and as I opened the door, the young man there thrust out his hand and said "Hey man! I am here about the job opening. Sounded good to me—kind of relaxed and no stress, hanging out with the B&B peeps."

Once more, I struggled for words as I beheld the young man's "professional attire." He was dressed (if you could call it that) in flip flops, old and frayed khaki cargo shorts, and then to top it all off, was wearing a Bud Light t-shirt that was cut off to give all viewers the opportunity to gaze at his ample and hairy belly that was bulging out over his belt. God forgive me, but before I could stop myself, I looked at him and smiled and then lied through my teeth, saying "I am so sorry; we have already filled the job. Thanks for coming by!" before I closed the door with a solid thump.

I went back to the desk and put my head in my hands. This finding help was not going to be as easy as I had thought. In my old world of business, there was an entire Human Resources department that recruited and vetted people, narrowing things down for me before the cream of the crop came in for interviews. Now there was no one between me and the great unwashed.

The doorbell rang again. With a sigh, I hauled

myself up and trudged over to answer the door, prepared for the worst and mentally resolving to not let anyone who looked as scary as the past two applicants even cross the threshold.

When I opened the door, I couldn't believe my eyes. Standing before me was an extraordinarily attractive young man, with beautiful green eyes, a haircut that made his blond hair look like a million dollars, and a flawless complexion--and even better, he had actually come for his interview dressed professionally in khakis, a dress shirt, and tie. With a big smile, he put out his hand with a firm handshake, and looking me in the eye said "Hi—my name is Alex, and I would be so honored if you could spare me a few moments for an interview. I had always admired this house, and it seems like it would be a great place to work." He was very personable, and I noticed on his resume that in addition to having worked as a waiter at several upscale restaurants, he had also worked briefly as a model for Abercrombie and Fitch. He was definitely the sharpest of the group that had applied, so despite his lack of B&B experience, I told him we would hire him for a two-week trial period, and figured our female guests would appreciate having someone ornamental around the premises.

I gave Alex the training packet to read and quizzed him on it the next day, and he was clearly a quick study. Before having him actually interact with guests, I decided to start him off in the behind-the-scenes part of the B&B, doing laundry, ironing, and cooking. The large kitchen/den area on the main floor was our work hub and private family space as well, and we made sure the doors were closed at all times and the guests oriented to avoid this private area, so that we could preserve the illusion that while we were having delightful conversations with guests and enjoying the finer things of life, the whole house stayed beautifully clean and the linens and towels immaculate and the flower arrangements refreshed without guests seeing the hard work on our part and that of our staff that kept the whole place running.

I left Alex with a large basket of linens that needed ironing and ran out to do some errands. When I came back, I walked into the kitchen, and there was Alex at the ironing board, with a big smile, but instead of linens he was ironing a very skimpy blouse, and there was an attractive young woman I had never seen before sitting there quite red in the face watching him. Since I had been out that morning, I figured she must be one of the guests who had just checked in. I was glad to see he was being helpful by ironing her blouse that had no doubt gotten wrinkled in her suitcase, but as I excused myself made a mental note to remind him later that guests were not allowed into the kitchen.

Later that afternoon I came back to the kitchen,

and Alex was still at the ironing board. The same young woman was still in the kitchen, too, even more red in the face. I noticed that she was now wearing the blouse Alex had been ironing before and that he was currently ironing some kind of garment that looked as if it had come from the racier section of Victoria's Secret. I felt very uncomfortable and asked Alex to come back to my office. I asked him to explain what was going on and why for the past two hours he had been ironing this woman's clothes, while I was paying him to iron the B&B's linen.

I explained I was all for helping guests out, but that this was going too far and that ironing "unmentionables" for guests was not really appropriate.

He said "Oh, that's OK. She's not a guest. She's one of my girlfriends, and well, she ....umm...she gets *into* it when I iron her clothes and she watches."

"So let me get this straight," I said. "While I am paying you to help us out in the B&B, you decided to invite one of your girlfriends to come over so you could use our iron and ironing board to iron her clothes in front of her because the two of you..umm..ENJOY that?"

"Yeah, that's right. I was going to get to the other stuff eventually." Looking up he looked me deeply in the eyes, and with a slow smile said "Maybe you have some special clothes you'd like me to iron for you while you watch? I'd be GLAD to do that for you."

"Thanks, Alex, but I don't really think so. You know, I just don't think this is going to work out. Why don't you take your … friend… and go ahead home? I'll send you a check, but you don't need to come back."

"Oh, OK, sorry, man. But you do have my number. Call me up if you want me to come over and do some, shall we say, *private* ironing for you. I'd LOVE to do that!" he said with a wink.

Fortunately, just at the moment that I was ready to despair of finding anyone to help us who would fit in at a G-rated bed and breakfast, there was a knock at the front door, and Sara Bader came into our lives. Sara was a college student wise beyond her years, a great cook, a great conversationalist, and had a wonderful knack for dealing with guests—she exuded a calming presence and we would soon learn that she was completely unflappable, no matter what happened.. Besides this, our children loved her, and she loved them right back. Even better, after her first few weeks of helping out, she recruited her friend Ryan to come work with us as well. Ryan was a huge help to me, as having another guy around to help haul the three-story ladder, move furniture around, repair doorknobs that guests would pull off, and re-hang pictures people knocked off the walls was a godsend. Ryan, too, was a natural at talking with and charming guests, and his affable, laid-back nature made him a pleasure to have around.

The two of them worked with us all the way through their college years and beyond, and we would never have made it without them. It may take a village to raise a child, but it takes great staff to keep a B&B owner sane.

November

L ike every season, autumn in Charleston has its own
particular charms. Sometime in November the
humidity finally gives out and you wake up to find clear
blue skies and a crisp coolness in the morning. One
unexpectedly delightful thing about Charleston, especially
in our neighborhood, is the large number of flowers which
bloom only in the fall.

My favorite is golden cassia, a shrub with spidery
foliage and cascades of brilliant yellow gold flowers. Under
the bright November sun with the azure sky above and
mellowed old brick walls in the background, they are truly
spectacular. Another favorite that blooms in the autumn is
the so-called Confederate rose, which actually looks more
like a hibiscus. There are several enormous specimens of
this tree-sized shrub within a block or two of our house,
and they always amaze tourists because each of the shrub's
very large blossoms is a slightly different color. The

blossoms start out white and gradually develop to a shade of pale pink before turning further to a dark reddish purple color in a way that seems nothing short of miraculous. Rounding out the autumnal display are the early sasanquas, elegant pink and red and white blossoms that look like porcelain surrounded by beautiful glossy green foliage. Given that the main botanical event of the fall in many cities is dead leaves, Charleston's floral abundance at this time of year seems an extravagant bonus from the Creator to an already heavenly locale.

We found that the city's slightly slower pace and agreeable weather in November attracted many guests to our bed and breakfast, which was ideally suited for walking everywhere, especially now that it was cool enough to not have to worry about heat stroke. In addition, guests at this time of year tended to be a bit older and more interested in the cultural side of Charleston, which made them a delight to have, as they especially appreciated the ambience and experience we were trying to offer. The downside was that all these fascinating conversations and interesting people made it difficult sometimes to carve out family time away from the guests.

One of the ironies of owning a bed and breakfast-- where you are providing a wonderful space for time away and relationship building for others—is that you often have to escape from the bed and breakfast to have your own time with your family. We were very fortunate early on in running the B&B to find a local restaurant that could serve as a bit of home away from home for us and our children. Jestine's Kitchen was opened by Dana Berlin a few years before we moved back to Charleston, and I had gone to eat there with my friend Preston during a visit shortly after they had opened.

I had known Dana slightly in high school and was delighted to see her again and loved the restaurant. It reminded me so much of growing up in Charleston, almost like going back to a Sunday night supper at my house or the house of friends. Jestine's is not fancy, but the food is delicious and authentically Lowcountry, and Dana and her staff are fabulous. Dana couples high standards, genuine warmth, and an amazing work ethic with an absolutely hilarious sense of humor.

My deep affection for Jestine's and for Dana and her crew was further enhanced while I was still working as an international business executive. I had put on a best practices conference at Charleston Place, one of Charleston's luxury hotels, where we had 50 or so CEOs and senior executives of billion dollar financial services companies attend from Argentina, Australia, France, Hong Kong, Italy, Japan, and South Africa. As I worked with our meetings department to plan a conference that would utilize to the fullest Charleston's unique venues, we planned amazing moments like a private plantation supper under a tent on the lawn at Middleton Place, following which we would be led by spirituals singers and torchlight to a dessert served by the butterfly lakes as musicians from the Charleston Symphony played chamber music. Another night we rode by carriage to a candlelight dinner in the ballroom where George Washington was entertained at the Old Exchange, and another evening had a fabulous sunset cocktail buffet at the Roper House, the High Battery home of financier Dick Jenrette, where Prince Charles had stayed during his visit to Charleston. As a counterpoint to these events, we organized one night of casual small dinners by country group in lesser-known but really good local restaurants. I decided to take the group from France to Jestine's.

During my visits with these gentlemen in Paris, I had had the privilege and pleasure of having a number of amazing lunches in the executive dining rooms of these companies, where often as not the company chef had come from a Michelin-starred restaurant and where very often the wine served came from a famous vineyard somewhere in France which the company owned outright or in which the company was a major investor. I knew that for these gentlemen, accustomed to dining out at Carré des Feuillants or Lucas Carton, the décor of Jestine's with its wooden tabletops without cloths and green washcloths rather than linen napkins would throw them for a loop and make them nervous. I also knew that unorthodox foods like okra and the very idea of Coca-Cola cake would cause them to sniff and look down their noses at this choice of restaurant. However, I was also supremely confident that, as is generally the case for most French people, the excellent quality of the cooking would overcome all these hurdles and that even before dessert they would be kissing the tips of their fingers in delight and noting the restaurant's *coordonnées* in their little black book of "*bonnes adresses.*"

Just as I predicted, when we walked in, there was a distinct murmuring from some of the Frenchmen looking around as Dana and her staff warmly welcomed us. There was more murmuring as I tried to translate various items on the menu—okra, collards, and hopping john are not things that would ever show up on a table in France, and cornbread is simply unimaginable to the French mind. They were good sports, though, and most of them let me order for them; their demeanor and the atmosphere were very like the feeling you have when you are waiting in line with a group of friends to get on a new rollercoaster and you're not quite sure whether it is going to be thrilling or terrifying or make you sick—or possibly all three. The food came out quickly, and things got very quiet. For Americans, that would be a bad sign, but for French people, that was encouraging—eating and appreciating good food is *sérieux*. Before long, the fried chicken and oysters and shrimp and fried okra and gumbo and cornbread had virtually disappeared, and I was being roundly congratulated on my choice of restaurant.

Now, as it was time for dessert, my suggestion that they at least try the Coca-Cola cake still met with some raised eyebrows. The idea of putting Coca-Cola, the *ne plus ultra* of American soft drinks, into a ....CAKE—really? I told them to trust me. As forks of the warm, moist, chocolaty cake with the perfect texture and the slightly hardened sweet caramel icing topped with a dollop of pure whipped cream met expectant taste buds, there were murmurs again—but this time of sublime delight. When Dana came back out to ask how everything was, the Frenchmen broke into spontaneous applause. The dinner was a triumph—great food, great service, great conversation, and the joy of new discoveries.

Ever since then, I had been a regular at Jestine's, and when we moved back to Charleston, we got in the habit of coming for Sunday dinner each week after church. Dana would always install us at the big round table in the back corner, and the children loved that they could get whatever they wanted since the prices were so reasonable. We would often show up for lunch or dinner on other days as well, especially when things were really busy in the B&B,

as we had learned that it doesn't really work to try to cook dinner for your four children in the same kitchen with one oven while your staff is at the same time trying to bake muffins, bread, and cake for breakfast. As a result, we got to know Dana and her staff really well, and they became like part of our family. Leigh would listen patiently to our stories of electrical and plumbing disasters that only seemed to occur when all our rooms were fully booked, and her brother Tyler, a genius at origami, would make wonderful toys for our children, including their favorite, a little dragon that you could cause to move by pulling on his tail. Belinda would always raise our spirits by putting "Santa Baby" on the stereo even in July and singing snatches of the song as she bustled around the restaurant cracking jokes with her keen wit. Dana helped raise our children, making sure that they behaved themselves, commenting when they were not properly dressed, and joking with them about what tortures they must be undergoing living in a B&B and being homeschooled by parents like us.

We all loved every minute of it, and these family times provided moments of reflection and insight on our new lifestyle in the bed and breakfast. When our daughter Amy was around six, we were sitting at the round table in the back corner at Jestine's after a delicious meal, and with a pensive expression, she looked at me for a moment and then said:

103

"Daddy, you know you used to fly all around the world and ride in limousines and make speeches and stuff, but now you don't do any of that."

"That's right, sweetie. Now I don't do that, and now I am here with you and our family all the time."

"Mm hmm, that's true. But what I really mean, is that now it's different...I mean, now you know a lot about TOILETS!"

Well, some days that did sort of seem to sum things up, and I did definitely know far more about toilets and fixing them than I had ever anticipated.

One day later that month, the doorbell rang at the B&B, and I looked out to see Dana's truck pulled up on the sidewalk and Dana with her arms full standing at the front door. I ran to open the door, and she said "I know you have all those starving children that you don't feed enough, and I am getting ready to close the restaurant for Thanksgiving. I had a bunch of desserts left over so I decided I would drop them off with you for the kids, if you would like to have them."

"Would we ever! That is so great—thank you SO much! The children will be thrilled," I said, walking her back to the kitchen. Soon the counter was covered with Coca-Cola cake, Black Magic cake, banana pudding, and pecan pie—guaranteed to result in a sugar-induced coma, but what a way to go.

"And there's one more in the truck. I've got to run, but hope you all have a wonderful Thanksgiving!"

"You too," I said, giving her a big hug as she handed me the last aluminum-foil covered pan. "Thanks for thinking of us—you are the best! The kids are going to be so excited. See you after the holidays!"

"Is that a promise or a threat?" she said with a big smile, and drove off waving as she tooted the horn.

Going back inside, I was curious which dessert was in the pan. As I took off the aluminum foil, I started laughing out loud. Dana had made my wife a special cake, knowing her birthday was coming up that weekend. Shaped like a giant boot, the chocolate cake had drawn on it many doors and windows, out of each of which were several children peering, and there was an inscription in icing that said "To the little old woman who lived in the shoe—she had so many children she didn't know what to do!" My wife and children had a good laugh when they saw it, and we and our visiting relatives made short work of all the desserts over the Thanksgiving holiday—and I said a silent prayer of thanks for all our friends at Jestine's.

The only drawback to Jestine's was that they were not open for breakfast, and especially on Saturday mornings where we had a full house at the B&B, which meant serving a full breakfast to between 12 and 16 people, it was hard to get too excited about making breakfast for the children while surrounded by heaps of dirty dishes and the detritus of the guests' meal. Fortunately, the Marina Variety Store, a fixture on the Charleston scene since the time I was growing up, was still around, and had not changed one bit in thirty years. It was only five minutes away, and met the highest culinary requirement of our children—they made excellent chocolate milk. Many a busy day at the B&B would find us at the Marina later in the morning with all four children, being waited on by Bambi, our favorite waitress, who kept the restaurant humming and always made sure our breakfasts were perfect and relaxing. She soon knew the names of all the children and what they would want to order, and we spent many happy hours snuggled together in a booth with a killer view of the Ashley River and every boat imaginable from simple Sunfish to mega-yachts. We would philosophize with Bambi about the hospitality business and the joys and trials of parenthood, while the children became experts on South Carolina geography by studying the placemats that featured a state map. And who couldn't love a restaurant where one of our favorite dishes was called Bear Island Specialty? November was indeed a time to count our blessings.

December

It was definitely a conundrum. All my life growing up in the Episcopal Church, I had been preached to numerous times about the value of keeping Advent, the season of preparation before the celebration of Christmas, and I have to admit to being a secret Advent "junkie"—I love the purple hangings and vestments, the austere Medieval Advent hymns with their minor keys and sense of building anticipation, the ceremony of the Advent wreath with its four candles, and the tradition of keeping the Twelve Days of Christmas, culminating in a Twelfth Night celebration on January 5, the eve of Epiphany.

The problem was that with every store in America starting to put up Christmas lights and playing Christmas music before they have even cleared the Halloween merchandise off the shelves, and "Grandma Got Run Over by a Reindeer" on every radio station, we were finding that most of our potential guests checking about reservations in December were all asking "Is your house decorated for Christmas?" And, clearly the right answer to the question from their perspective was "Of course!"

I had actually been looking forward to decorating this wonderful house for Christmas in true Charleston style, with fragrant boughs of evergreens, garlands of smilax, topiaries with boxwood and lemons and oranges, mistletoe, and lots of magnolia leaves, but I had not anticipated starting the weekend of Thanksgiving, which was when guests seemed to expect it. We had always waited in my family until at least the third or fourth week of Advent before decorating, and it just seemed far too early to start.

Besides tradition, a major force in anyone's blood in Charleston, another issue was that all these beautiful natural decorations would be dry tinder for a brush fire long before Christmas, let alone Twelfth Night, if we decorated this early. My wife and I discussed it, and she pointed out that I really did enjoy decorating for Christmas, so why not double my pleasure and do it twice—right after Thanksgiving and then again after the middle of December? I could try different things and different materials, and it might be fun. As usual, she was right, and I realized it could actually be a source of joy.

So, on the first day of December just after Thanksgiving break, I got up early and found my little saw, several pairs of garden shears, and a couple of laundry baskets, and piled it all in my Volvo station wagon. Putting some Advent choral music on the car stereo (perhaps to assuage that little twinge of guilt for starting so early), I headed out to my friend Preston's country property, where he had told me I could cut away to my heart's content. There was virtually no traffic as I headed out of the city, and in fifteen minutes I was pulling up at the gate to Preston's land. Unlocking the bolt, I headed down the narrow, rutted lane and was soon immersed in the otherworldly beauty of the Lowcountry in December.

Gnarled old live oaks dripping with Spanish moss overhung the lane, and through the boughs you could see the marsh and tidal creek with little ghosts of mist hovering in the air as the sun began peeking through the tree canopy. Birds were calling everywhere, and occasionally I would spot a graceful deer motionless in the woods waiting for me to pass. Other than the birds, the silence was complete, as if I were all alone in a newly made world.

The Lowcountry landscape speaks into your soul, and on this morning, I could see how Archibald Rutledge and other writers like him had been inspired to write hundreds of pages as a paean to the beauty that surrounds the outdoorsman in this part of the world. One of the incredible things about Charleston is that you can leave downtown and in fifteen minutes be somewhere that feels unimaginably remote and disconnected from the frenetic pace of our wired-in world.

I stopped the car before the lane deteriorated into a bog and started walking through the woods with all my paraphernalia and clippers. Feeling a bit like a child in a candy shop, I chopped and chopped—gorgeous boughs of holly laden with bright red berries that the birds had not gotten yet, shiny smilax with its little brown tendrils that made it easy to hang around the house, big branches of brownleaf magnolia that is glossy green on one side and velvety brown on the other, tallow tree branches known in Charleston as popcorn tree for their white berries, and fragrant cedar branches that were used in the Lowcountry in place of the fir and spruce that could never grow in our semi-tropical heat. After years of frustration at the lack of things to cut in my Buckhead yard back in Atlanta when I was decorating for Christmas, I was delighted to be here in the Ali Baba's cave of Christmas greenery, surrounded with unimaginable riches, all mine for the taking.

After I had filled up all my baskets, I decided it was time to load back up and go look for a Christmas tree at one of the lots I had seen downtown. I was already resigned to the fact that I was probably going to have to put up and decorate a tree in the sure and certain knowledge that I would be taking it down before Christmas, removing all the ornaments and lights, and putting up another. I went back to the house and unloaded the greenery and filled up the back seat with my children to get their help with selecting the tree.

Whit, prescient even as a seven-year-old, asked tentatively "Daddy, isn't it a little...umm...early to be getting a tree? I mean, we just had Thanksgiving and you always talk about how awful it is that people are rushing Christmas." Well, my own words were coming back to haunt me, so I reached for a classic and responded with Charles Dickens "'I will honor Christmas in my heart'— but the B&B guests want some decorations, so we are going to put some up for them". That was all the encouragement the children needed to go into giddy anticipation of having the tree up and decorated early—and who knows, maybe an early visit from Santa as well.

Now, getting a Christmas tree is a process laden with cultural layers and expectations and family traditions—you could spend months doing psycho-analysis of poor Charlie Brown's travails in choosing a tree—and I am afraid I have some quirks in this area as well. Every Christmas when I was a small child, my grandparents had an enormous and fragrant cedar as their Christmas tree, freshly cut from my grandmother's plantation. The red cedar (which is actually a beautiful

111

shade of green) is a classic Christmas tree in much of the South, where more traditional (i.e., Northern) evergreen trees don't grow. Cedars are not so easy to find in tree lots, but I had spotted a lot near the grocery store downtown that had some. The children and I went to the lot and picked the tallest cedar they had, which would barely fit on top of the Volvo, and we got ready to tie it on.

Whit, putting his hands on his hips, looked up at me and said with immense moral authority "Don't forget what happened last year. We certainly don't want THAT to happen again, do we? I know I don't!"

My mind flashed back to last Christmas in Atlanta, when Whit and I had gone out to get the Christmas tree and had ended up having a traumatic evening. Having just returned from a long trip to Asia, I had decided I needed some father/son time with Whit, so as soon as I got back from the airport, despite my jet lag, I had suggested that we guys go get the tree and then get dinner at Fellini's Pizza on Peachtree Road, which Whit loved. We went to the tree lot in Buckhead and wandered around, but could not find any cedars. Disappointed, but knowing Whit would get worn out if we went from lot to lot searching for one, I decided that I would let him pick among the beautiful and very fresh Fraser firs arrayed under the strings of white lights. He picked a great tree, and the very helpful young man at the lot said he would carry the tree to our car and assured me he would tie it on securely for us so we wouldn't lose it in traffic. I had mentioned that last year our Christmas tree had come off the roof of the car on Peachtree Street right in front of Piedmont Hospital and that it had nearly caused multiple accidents and that I had narrowly avoided being run over. He said he understood and would make sure it would not come off until we got home. Whit and I got into the car, and the young man put the great-smelling tree on the roof and had us opening and closing doors and windows and the sunroof, passing various ropes through and getting us to hand them to him on the other side. From the crisscross of ropes across the ceiling, I figured it looked pretty safe, so I gave him a good tip and headed with Whit to Fellini's.

Coming in the back way through Garden Hills, we pulled into the downhill parking area behind the restaurant, and that was when our troubles began.

"Daddy," said Whit, "my door is stuck." This happened sometimes with the back door in the Volvo, so I told him to push into it a little with his elbow.

He pushed again and said "Nope—it's not budging."

"Don't worry, buddy. I'll hop out and open it from the outside. I can smell the pizza from here—this is going to be great," I said, looking at the twinkling lights decorating the restaurant and looking forward to a fun dinner with my son. Pushing the door handle to hop out and set Whit free, I was surprised to find that my door was sticking as well. My door had never stuck before, so this was surprising. I threw my shoulder into it, but it would not budge. I was perplexed—had something with the remote locking system malfunctioned? What could this be?

Seconds later, Whit figured it out. "Daddy, I was afraid of this. That boy at the tree lot you liked so much because he was making the tree so secure? Well, I was watching and I thought he tied the doors closed. Now I am sure he did. That's why we can't open them. Look at how those ropes are in the windows. He tied us in here! That's pretty funny—I thought you would have said something. Ha ha—we are stuck in our own car! Tied up! Ha ha—this is like something that would happen in the movies!"

Well, I have to say Whit was enjoying this much more than I was, as I realized he was exactly right about what had happened and I was kicking myself mentally for having been too dense to notice that I was being tied up in my own car by this well-meaning but clearly obtuse young man.

Now the trick was how to get out. With all the ropes through the windows there was not much room, but clearly that was our only option. I got Whit to climb up to the front seat and then fed his head and body out through the driver's window until he could grab onto the tree on top of the car, and then told him to pull his legs out and then drop. He negotiated all this like a pro, and soon was standing on the street, saying "Come on, Daddy—you can do it!"

By this point, a small crowd of bystanders had gathered who had been enjoying Happy Hour at a neighboring bar, and they thought the spectacle was hilarious, as they laughed and made comments about the poor sap who was too dumb to realize he was being tied up in his own car. I had managed to get my head and shoulders out, but was now wedged pretty firmly in the window and didn't seem to be able to move.

Now the guffaws got louder "Look, now he's stuck in his own window—and in a business suit too! "

To his immense credit, Whit was ignoring the onlookers, refusing to make fun of me even when I looked ridiculous, and continuing to encourage me. "Come on— you're almost there! Grab the trunk of the tree with your hand and pull yourself through!"

I reached my hand up and then CRAACK— simultaneously a large branch of the tree broke off and I popped out of the window, landing in a heap on the road, to the great amusement of all. We slinked into the restaurant and Whit looked me in the eye and said "Daddy, don't ever go get a tree without me. You need help!"

Leaving memory lane and coming back to

Charleston, I wholeheartedly agreed that Whit was right—we did not want that to happen again! I made sure all the doors were open as we tied the tree on, and as we headed back down South of Broad, the children were excited about putting the tree up. We got the tree off the roof and carried it into the house, where I had left a stand in the corner of the Drawing Room. Positioning the tree in the stand, I stepped back to admire it and wondered why the children were being so quiet. As I stood back and looked up, I too was silent—we definitely had a problem.

Our Drawing Room looked like an ad for a new movie entitled "Honey, I Shrunk the Christmas Tree." Although this tree had been the tallest cedar on the lot, its 8 foot height was dwarfed by our 15 foot ceilings and the size of the room. It looked positively Lilliputian.

"Don't worry, kids," I said, putting on a brave smile, "We'll put this one upstairs and get a bigger one for down here. I know where I can go cut one down that we can put in the Drawing Room that will look way better than this."

Looking up at me with a knowing smile, Whit said "Well, I'm coming with you. Remember what happened last year."

Heading back to the car, we made the hour-long trek out the Savannah Highway in afternoon traffic to Yonges Island and Toogoodoo Christmas Tree Farm, for which I had seen an ad in the paper. The farm, named after the Toogoodoo River which it borders, features Toogie the Talking Christmas Tree as well as the Toogoodoo ChooChoo (try saying that three times in a row really quickly!) and has a great selection of big trees. Although it is a "cut your own tree" kind of place, I had heard that sometimes when it is not too busy you could get someone to help you.

Pulling into the dirt road, we saw it was a beautiful place—loads of trees and the late afternoon sun coming through in long angled rays of golden light. We found the cedars, and I was soon using the measuring stick to try to guesstimate which of the ones Whit and I liked would be tall enough to look right in the Drawing Room. Picking the most likely candidate, I lay down under the tree and began sawing. I sawed and sawed but had only made it through perhaps 1/8 of the truck. I crawled out, wiped off the dirt and bugs, and crawled under the other side of the tree to begin sawing again.

True to form, Whit yelled out some encouragement "You're doing a great job, Daddy! Don't let the tree beat you!" I sawed and sawed, but the trunk just seemed enormous. I was starting to feel red in the face and my arms were growing numb, but I was determined not to give up. Panting as I sawed, I noticed a pair of shoes walking my direction and soon heard a voice calling out to me.

"Sir? Sir? Can I help you with that?"

Dragging myself back out, I was delighted to see a smiling young man carrying a large saw and wearing a Toogoodoo shirt. He said "I'd be happy to get this one down for you." I readily assented and figured Whit and I could walk around for 15 or 20 minutes while he finished cutting it down. We started off towards a grove of trees when I heard a rushing sound and a thump—our tree was down, and it had only taken him three minutes. Trying to make me feel better, Whit took my hand and said "Don't worry, Daddy—he's still young."

We got the tree back over to the car on the tractor, the Toogoodoo crew rolled the tree onto the roof of the car, and we soon realized we had another problem. Whit went around and opened all the doors of the car, ensuring we weren't going to get tied in, but none of us could think of a solution for the fact that the tree was longer than the car. The front part of it drooped off the roof, covering the windshield and the hood of the car. We eventually decided to use a net to pull the tree backwards and have it hang off the back rather than the front. That seemed like a good plan, so we got the tree tied down and Whit and I headed back to town.

As we drove back down Hwy. 17 to Charleston, I noticed a lot of people were staring at the car. It was a really, really big tree and did look pretty funny on top of the car. Just before we got back to downtown Charleston, we had to stop suddenly for a car that pulled out without looking, and suddenly the windshield was a mass of green. The tree had slipped out of its net and was covering the windshield again. I was not about to get out of the car and try to drag the tree back up since we were only two miles from home, so I said to Whit "Don't worry; I am sure with using the windshield wipers I will be able to see just fine." Whit didn't reply—he had his eyes closed tight, and I am pretty sure he was praying.

The windshield wipers did allow me to get an occasional look at the road, and with the various mirrors and an occasional look from popping my head out the window, we finally managed to get back to our house. Getting out of the car, we noticed that the tree seemed to have grown—it really looked big now that we had it at the house. I got Ryan, our afternoon innkeeper, to come out and help me with the tree, and he turned pale when he came out and saw it.

"I think we're going to need some help," he said. "That thing is enormous!"

I cut the ropes on the tree and said "Let's roll it off the car." With Ryan's help, we rolled it off the car, but unfortunately it was too wide to drop down to the sidewalk as I had intended, and instead the tree was impaled in multiple places on the wrought iron fence in front of our house. I moved the car away and was now confronted by the strange spectacle of a large cedar tree lying sideways on top of a wrought iron fence.

Help clearly was a good idea. I started calling friends, neighbors, everyone I could think of, but hardly anyone was available. Eventually we found a tourist off the street, a neighbor, and the rector of our church ("Here comes the Advent guilt again", I thought), and we were able to manhandle the tree through the front door and into the Drawing Room. It was every bit of 15 feet tall but was also about 6 feet wide.

It smelled great, though, and I was sure it would look great once we stood it up. I put the stand on while the tree was on its side, and we began to lift to set the tree upright in the corner, the idea being that you could see it out of the front and side windows of the Drawing Room. "Began" is the operative word here, because every time we would get past a 45 degree angle with the tree, its sheer weight would push all of us sliding back down over the polished floors of the Drawing Room. Eventually, we had to get the 15 foot step ladder and rig a pulley so that we could haul the tree upright. Because it still seemed unsteady, we tied it down to a hook on the ceiling and to hooks on the adjacent windows.

It had now been well over two hours since we had pulled the tree off the fence. Decorating was going to have to wait for the next day. I profusely thanked our friends who had helped, and was grateful the rector had not made any cracks about putting up a Christmas tree during the first week of Advent.

I followed Ryan back into the kitchen to get something to drink. He had been a trooper through the whole thing, standing in the middle of the tree as we tried to stand it up. He looked at me and said "I don't feel so great" and showed me his arms, which were covered with big red welts. At first I thought they were just scratches from all the branches, but then he pulled up his shirt and we saw his chest and back were covered with red welts as well. "I think I'm allergic to this kind of tree," he said. Fortunately, after a good dose of Benadryl, the welts started to fade, and even better, Ryan didn't decide to quit after the experience.

Once we had the lights on and the ornaments on the tree, it looked truly spectacular. The boughs of green on the mantelpieces with the vibrant holly berries, the shiny magnolia and fragrant cedar, and the rich smell of the fruit topiaries and bayberry candles created a sense that you had stepped back a few centuries into an earlier Christmas. Our guests absolutely loved it, and as we bade the last of them farewell as we closed for three days starting Christmas Eve, our whole family fell under the spell of the beauty of this season.

We decided to walk to the midnight service at St. Philip's, letting the children sleep until the last minute, and then waking them and helping them into their beautiful hand-smocked Christmas outfits. It was a brisk but not uncomfortable night with a bright full moon, and as we walked past cobblestone streets and windows of 18th century houses lit with candles and hung with beautiful wreaths of fragrant green branches on the doors, and heard snatches of Christmas hymns as we walked past the two churches we passed along the way, we all felt a sense of joy to be in this place.

Just as we got to St. Philip's and were ushered through the massive doors into the beauty and warmth of the church, the peals began from the steeple bells and the choir in its traditional English vestments broke into the ancient a cappella plainchant anthem "Hodie Christus natus est," which reverberated and echoed through the incredible acoustics of the narthex, sounding like an angelic host and causing the children's eyes to open wide in wonder. What a blessed place to call home at Christmas!

January

Much as we were loving our new life in the bed and breakfast, we were also craving some time to escape—time where we did not have to worry about whether the breakfast staff person was actually going to show up, time when we would not have to answer the 2 a.m. phone call to explain how the Jacuzzi works, time to read a good book uninterrupted. After a wonderful first Christmas in our new home, we had been given the most beautiful gift of all: my longsuffering parents had offered to come run the bed and breakfast for a few weeks so we could have some time away. They would come after New Year's weekend, and we would escape with the children to Europe for a few weeks with friends there.

We were booked solid for New Year's, mostly with folks from New York, and before we left town we were looking forward to doing a big champagne breakfast for our guests, adding to our usual menu our own recipes for Hoppin' John and collard greens, two staples of Lowcountry fare for New Year's, guaranteed to bring good luck and prosperity. We figured we could use all the luck and prosperity we could get, and were happy to set up our guests for success as well.

The last of the New Year's guests to arrive was Sonja, a thirty-something angst-ridden woman from New York City, coming for the New Year's weekend because she said her nerves were shot and she really needed to get away. She told us on the phone that she could not wait to get to the B&B because Manhattan was making her crazy and she desperately needed to go somewhere quiet to regroup. We assured her that our B&B was indeed quiet and that we sought to cultivate an atmosphere of calm and peace. She called us every day in the week leading up to her stay, wanting us to reassure her that the B&B in general and the room we had assigned her were quiet and peaceful.

Finally, the night came for her to arrive, and she called to let us know that the airline was torturing her and her nerves, that her flight had been delayed numerous times and that now she was not slated to arrive until around one in the morning. She asked if we could possibly leave a check-in packet and a key for her so she would not wake up the whole place when she arrived, to which we happily agreed.

When we got up the next morning, we saw the packet was gone and figured we would see Sonja at breakfast. Shortly before breakfast was over, a Garbo-esque figure clad in black from head to toe appeared in the entrance hall, wearing dark sunglasses and stiletto heels, with her hair wrapped up in a black silk scarf, an effect made all the more dramatic by her blood-red lipstick and nail polish. She stumbled in my direction, took my hand, and looking me in the eye said "I am Sonja, dear. Charmed to meet you, I'm sure. I am so sorry, dear, but I am going to have to check out right away."

I told her how sorry I was to hear that and asked if there was anything we could do to help and if there was any problem with the room.

She said she loved the B&B and how beautiful everything was, but that she had lain awake all night with her nerves bothering her because it was too quiet—FAR too quiet for someone from New York to be able to sleep. She then said "...and the LIGHT--all that light was so BRIGHT. I couldn't sleep at all."

Perplexed, I asked what light she meant, and she said "the light from the MOON--it was so bright through the windows. You should do something about all those windows. Get window shades and curtains. You know, we know how to manage these things in New York." (Reader's Note: there were already opaque window shades and curtains on all the windows in her room—apparently it had not occurred to her to close them).

At this point, she asked if we could get her a reservation at the Hampton Inn; she had seen it from the taxi driving in and thought it looked like it wouldn't be so quiet, and maybe there would be enough noise for her to sleep.

As the taxi we had called her pulled up, she was practically in tears, hugging me and apologizing, saying "everything is so beautiful here, everything is SO nice, I just can't BEAR to leave, I mean I just LOVE it here, such a wonderful place, but I have to go--my NERVES! the LIGHT!"

Watching the taxi speed away to the Hampton Inn, I figured that was the last we would hear of Sonja, but much to our surprise, she told all of her friends in New York that she had never stayed in such a great place as our B&B, and many of them came to see us and became loyal regular guests. All of them seemed to have figured out how to close the shades...

The blessed day finally arrived when my parents pulled up in their car to begin their stint as innkeepers. I knew they would do a great job, as both of them have engaging personalities and are by nature cheerful and helpful, and my mother particularly has a deep knowledge of Charleston history and architecture and horticulture. We had left them notebooks full of information, lots of phone numbers for repair people, and notes on all the incoming guests. They assured us they had everything under control and bundled us out the door to the airport.

While my parents were minding the B&B, they had several long chats on the reservations line with a man named Nubert, who was a construction worker from rural Alabama trying to plan a trip that would be the honeymoon he and his bride Wyolene had never been able to have when they got married a few years back. He had never stayed in a B&B before but thought his wife would like our place.

My mother was very impressed with how thoughtful he was on the phone and tried to put him at ease, as he seemed a little intimidated about staying somewhere so upscale. Finally, the day came when Nubert and Wyolene were to arrive to stay in the Ginkgo Suite, one of our prettiest rooms, which was painted a sunny yellow and decorated with our collection of blue and white porcelain, and had a beautiful fireplace and a Jacuzzi bath as well.

Odessa, the housekeeper, had been acting strange all morning, murmuring and giggling to herself and singing in a loud voice while she was in the laundry room. She had on an especially strong dose of perfume, and whenever she came through the room it was just about enough to make your eyes water. Mother thought to herself that perhaps she should say something to her, but then thought that it was important to stay on Odessa's good side, and at least it seemed she was enjoying her work. She seemed to have gotten a lot done that morning, and had told Mother she had gotten all the rooms made up and ready for the day's check-ins.

Mother asked Odessa to go back and make sure that Ginkgo was thoroughly clean and ready for Nubert and Wyolene, and then asked her to take back to the room two special flower arrangements filled with fragrant blossoms that Mother had made just to be nice.

Let's listen in as Nubert and Wyolene arrive.

"Oh my, Nubert, this is the most beautiful place I have ever seen! Are we really staying here?"

"Sho' nuff, honey. We are going to be living large for a few days."

"Oh my—just look at all these antiques and these beautiful flowers. Nubert, you are just the sweetest thing EVER. I am so happy I could just squeal!"

Well, thankfully Wyolene kept the squeal to herself, and seeing that they were all settled (and keeping the secret that she was responsible for the flowers, not Nubert), Mother excused herself after giving Nubert a card with the directions to the restaurant where they had dinner reservations. It was always nice to have satisfied guests.

Later that evening, my parents were relaxing in the drawing room, enjoying the decanter of sherry and a good book. Around eleven o'clock, Mother heard some light tapping but thought it was just another one of the noises old houses sometimes make. However, the tapping became a little louder, and looking up, she could see through the drawing room window that Nubert was up on the back porch tapping on the back door.

She went to the door and invited him in, noticing that he was all dressed up in a vest and string tie and some kind of boots, and that he seemed rather anxious and jumpy and kept averting his eyes.

"Hello, Nubert. Don't you look nice! I hope you and Wyolene had a nice dinner."

"Oh yes ma'am. It was delicious and all the folks were so nice to us. We had a grand time."

Nubert continued to stand there, shifting his weight back and forth from one side to another and mumbling slightly under his breath while looking down at his boots.

"Umm, umm…"

"Nubert, is there anything wrong? Is there something we can do to help? We are so happy that you and Wyolene are here with us. How can we help?"

Nubert looked up, his eyes starting to water and said "Oh ma'am, y'all have jest been so nice and lovely to me and Wyolene and this place is just beautiful. I jest don't know, I mean, we have never been anywhere before; we are more likely to be at Ryan's and Motel 6 and we jest don't know how folks do things in these here fancy establishments…"

"Well Nubert, we are delighted to have you and Wyolene. You just be yourselves and I am sure everything will be fine."

"Yes ma'am, I am sure you are right. It's just…, well, I jest don't know how to say it; I jest didn't know…Oh my, what am I going to do? I am so embarrassed."

"Why Nubert, whatever is wrong, I am sure we can help."

"Well, ma'am, I ain't never stayed in a B&B before, and it is so lovely and all, but I jest didn't know and I don't rightly know what to do. Oh my my…"

"Nubert, what didn't you know? I am sure we can help—just let me know what the problem is."

"Oh ma'am, I am just so embarrassed because I didn't know and I should have asked. Wyolene didn't know either, though, and we just don't know, I mean, what in the world are we going to do? What are we going to do? We have got ourselves into some fix now, and I am kickin' myself because I guess I should've asked, but I just did not know. My oh my."

"Didn't know what, Nubert?"

Nubert leaned over, looked around to ensure no one was watching, and in a breathy whisper just next to Mother's ear said "We didn't know we were supposed to bring our own SHEETS!"

Somewhat nonplussed, Mother said "But whatever do you mean? What are you talking about?"

"Well, ma'am, it is just embarrassing, because we did not know. We ain't never been to a B&B and we thought that sheets were, you know,... _included_ in the price. If we'd a-known, we would have brought some from home, and now here we are late at night, and y'all have been so lovely to us, and we got all those purty flowers you put in there, but we don't have no sheets and Wyolene is fit to be tied and I jest feel dumb because I didn't ask and it is all my fault. Oh my, oh my, I do not know what in the Sam Hill to do about it, because it is late and there is nowhere we can get us a sheet at this hour."

"Nubert, are you trying to tell me there are no sheets on your bed?"

"No ma'am, I mean, yes ma'am, there is nary a sheet in sight and I do apologize, I just did not know we were supposed to bring our own sheets. We pulled back the comforter and there was the mattress, and I mean it looks like a real nice mattress and everything but there just ain't a sheet. And I know I should have brought some, and I do apologize, I do indeed."

Mother, horrified that Odessa had somehow managed to make up the bed but neglected to put on sheets, patted him on the back and said "My dear man, do not think one more moment about it—we have plenty of sheets and I will right this minute come out and put them on for you. They should have been on the bed in the first place."

Nubert's face broke into a broad smile as his worries fled away. "Oh ma'am, that is just great news! You folks are just the nicest, kindest people, and I do apologize; we just did not know. I will be happy to pay the sheet rental fee. But please, ma'am, do NOT come back there. Wyolene has already got on her special nightgown, don't you know, and I think it might be better if you just let me take the sheets on back there myself."

"Nubert, there is no sheet rental fee—we are happy for you to have the sheets. I feel like the least I could do is to make up the bed for you, but I do not want to intrude on your privacy. Are you sure you will be able to make up the bed yourself?"

"Oh yes ma'am, no doubt, Wyolene and I can handle it jest fine. I will just take these beautiful sheets on back there. You are just so kind, and I thank you very kindly. Oh, and by the way, I mean, if there is an extra charge for havin' sheets, I would be happy to pay whatever, especially after putting you to all this trouble, with it bein' so late and all."

"No, Nubert—no extra charge; the sheets are on the house. You and Wyolene have a good night. We will look forward to seeing you at breakfast!"

"Oh ma'am, thank you so much. I just didn't know; I do apologize for all the trouble. Lordy, Wyolene will be so happy to see these sheets. We will take good care of them for you. Good night now!"

Upon hearing this story when we got back, we realized that my parents were naturals at innkeeping—they had carried off a difficult and embarrassing situation with great aplomb. We said we would be glad to have them come back and innsit anytime they would like.

With a twinkle in her eye, my mother looked at me smiling and said "Running the bed and breakfast for y'all was great, but it was truly a once in a lifetime experience—emphasis on the "ONCE"!" I always knew my mother was a smart woman.

February

February days in Charleston can be either like a gift from the gods with clear blue skies, no humidity, and the promise of spring, or they can be like a storm scene from a Herman Melville or Patrick O'Brian novel with sheets of rain, howling wind, and old wooden houses that feel as if they are pitching like ships as an old-fashioned nor'easter breaks over the city. When the weather falls into the latter category, having "a little something" to warm the bones definitely improves one's outlook. We had decided early on with the bed and breakfast that we would serve sherry in the late afternoon, and our guests found this to be a delightful custom.

Sherry has always been popular in Charleston, and I daresay that our South of Broad Street neighborhood probably has the highest proportion of sherry decanters in active use of any location in North America. When I was a callow youth working for one of the historical societies in Charleston, I was always interested by the presence of a large sherry decanter in the waiting room of one of the house museums. I soon learned that this decanter was in great demand, as the volunteer docents would linger in this room waiting for tourists to guide through the house. In the grand tradition of Charleston sociability, these ladies of a certain age would have a little tipple while catching up on the latest gossip. The most interesting tours of the house were always the last ones of the day given by docents who had been on duty by the sherry decanter through the languid hours of the afternoon. You not only learned about the glorious past as reflected in the furniture and the architecture, but also all about the seamy present--who was doing what with whom in the modern comfort of air conditioning.

Recalling all that delightful sociability, I had decided that serving sherry should be a key part of our guests' Charleston experience. We had decided that shooting sherry was a more authentic taste of Charleston than the ubiquitous Harvey's Bristol Cream, and we had made various trips up to the liquor store conveniently just across the street from the grocery in search of the perfect brand selection. Christine, the proprietor, helped us with various selections of amontillados and other exotic sherries, all the while telling us we should try Taylor's Golden. We resisted, since Taylor's did not sound exotic enough, until the day when we had run out of an expensive amontillado and served Taylor's the next day to some British guests who were sherry aficionados. They proclaimed the Taylor's far better than the other, and since it was half the price, we decided to switch brands. My wife, who was usually doing errands with our daughter Mary Hollis (age four at the time) in tow, soon discovered that the liquor store was one of Mary Hollis's favorite destinations. Not only was it across from the grocery which had free cookies, but the liquor store had a great candy jar as well as a cute small dog.

Every time my wife went to buy sherry, Mary Hollis wanted to go. However, this soon created embarrassing situations, such as the time while my wife was at a ladies' meeting at church. Mary Hollis came running up, clutching at her mother's skirt and exclaiming in a loud voice "Mommy! Mommy! I want you to take me to the liquor store again, Mommy! I want to go to the liquor store NOW!"

But I digress...

On the days that our sherry supply ran low when we were making trays up for turndown service, we would fill the little decanters on the old blue and white porcelain plates with Cointreau or Armagnac or brandy from our private stock. Guests were usually delighted, and it saved us from having to make desperate just-before-sundown runs to the liquor store for more sherry. The little turndown trays featured not only sherry with two sherry flutes, but also a scattering of benne wafers, a traditional Charleston confection of benne seeds.

I should explain that, for those who are "from off", benne is the Gullah word for sesame, and I believe there is some truth in the story that this recipe for benne wafers came from Africa with the slaves, whose cooking traditions became one of the dominant forces in the evolution of Lowcountry cuisine. Benne wafers are supposed to bring good luck, so we served them at every available opportunity.

One evening when I went back to prepare the trays, I found that there was only the scent of sherry left in the bottle--nary a drop of the real thing. Since we were out of sherry and Christine always closes the liquor store right on time, I decided to dip into my personal stock of Cointreau for that evening's turndown libation. I filled the decanters up, placed the little labels indicating Cointreau and Charleston Benne Wafers, and summoned our innkeeper to take the trays to the rooms.

Taking the trays to the rooms was one of the daily moments of high drama in the life of the bed and breakfast, rather like a very suspenseful film where you continually hold your breath as you hope against hope that the hero or heroine will make the death-defying leap and land in safety. To take the trays to the guestrooms without incident meant running a challenging gauntlet. Take one century-old blue and white porcelain plate, balance on it a small decanter and two top-heavy crystal sherry glasses, add one paper label in script, and a half dozen benne wafers, and you're ready for adventure.

First you have to get out of the kitchen, going out the door (where the 18th century doorknob usually fails to function, often requiring a body block to open the door), climbing up one stair, then down another to the entrance hall, through the hall door to the Hall of a Thousand Doors (actually there are five doors in a space that is 3 feet square--this is what real estate agents call "charm") to the back door. The back door sticks badly when it is humid (only 360 days a year), so you have to balance the tray and its contents with one hand while with the other hand you yank on the door handle with all your might.

If you succeed in getting the back door open without outside assistance, and if none of our children come barreling in and knock you over, then you have to contend with the screened door, which is mounted backwards (more "charm"), leaving you a narrow little angle where if you push with your back you can just manage to get out to the piazza and turn around so that you don't have to go down the piazza steps backwards. As you make your way gingerly down the stairs, you have to simultaneously avoid colliding with the window box and the light fixture mounted too low, while at the same time trying to keep the scripted label and any small benne wafers from becoming airborne from the piazza's ceiling fans.

Once you've reached the bottom of the piazza steps, you must navigate across the terrace in the dark, taking care not to slip on any mossy bricks, while with one hand you balance the tray and with the other search your pockets for the small stuffed animal key ring that will allow you to unlock the guestrooms. Having found the correct key, you again balance the tray with one hand while you try to get the correct key in at the correct angle to open the door, while at the same time knocking decorously but firmly to warn the guests of your approach so as to avoid the mutual embarrassment of catching anyone in a state of *deshabille* or worse.

Having satisfied yourself that the coast is clear, you open the door with one hand while balancing the tray on the other, only to find that the table where you usually put the turndown tray is covered with 300 bottles of different cosmetics.

At this point, you have several choices: you can throw the tray in the air and run screaming in the other direction, you can gamble that the mattress is firm and place the tray on the bed while you clear the table (the downside being that the decanter may turn over, in which case you will have to strip and remake the bed, not to mention start all over with the turndown tray), or you can put the tray on the floor and hope that you are sufficiently lithe and coordinated not to spill it in the downward or upward trajectory.

Who says that there's no adventure in the life of a B&B owner--or housekeeper, as we'll see in a moment? Very few careers other than brain surgery afford the opportunity for such feats of dexterity as those described above. You may have noticed one repeated phrase in this scenario from which we learned again the folly of taking any seemingly simple task for granted, that phrase being *"while balancing the tray with the other hand."*

We discovered that in fact it is very difficult to balance such a tray with one hand, which is a primary reason why after having destroyed a service for twenty of blue and white porcelain, not to mention a case of sherry glasses, we decided it might be a better idea to invite the guests to come to the Drawing Room for their sherry and benne wafers.

Well, I know you are wondering what happened with the Cointreau. We had some very prosperous guests who had been with us several days, and it was their last night in Charleston. They had reserved a limousine the next morning to take them to a friend's plantation for several days of shooting, so I figured they would appreciate the fact that we were giving them a nice treat with the Cointreau. When they came down for breakfast in the morning, I greeted them in the Drawing Room, whereupon the man grinned and said to me "That was a pretty good trick you played with the Cointreau last night."

"What kind of trick do you mean?" I asked, trying to figure out what he meant. Maybe the decanter had turned over when I closed the door? Had a palmetto bug made a kamikaze dive into their drink?

"Well," he said, "I thought it was a pretty clever money-saving device to put a label that says "Cointreau" on a decanter full of water. That really takes guts!"

"Sir," I said, "I am so sorry, but I'm not following you. Are you saying that your turndown tray decanter was full of WATER instead of Cointreau?"

"You got it, sport. Pretty good trick, I say. Didn't bother us, though, not after all the wine we had with dinner, but thought you'd like to know."

After apologizing profusely and turning the guests over to our morning innkeeper for breakfast, I scurried back to the pantry and pulled down my very large, very expensive bottle of Cointreau. Opening it up, I was reassured by the faint scent of orange that the liqueur gives off, until I realized that the scent was faint because only the bottle top had any residue of Cointreau left; the entire bottle was full of water.

As I wondered what could have happened, my mind reached back to several peculiar incidents that occurred last month while my parents were running the bed and breakfast for us. They had had a lot of trouble with the housekeeper, Odessa, whom they had eventually had to let go.

The most troubling incident for my mother was the morning that she was sitting on the piazza having a well-deserved moment of tranquility reading, after several hours of arranging flowers. She had given Odessa the day's instructions, and the housekeeper was supposed to be turning over rooms.

Odessa walked out onto the piazza, sat down, put her feet up, smacked Mother's book, and said in a belligerent voice "I see you taking a load off and reading. I'm goin' to bring my book tomorrow and sit out here all day long an' read, just like you. I need to ree-lax. Let these rooms clean up themselves."

Mother, somewhat taken aback, decided the best course of action was to just nod her head and see where this was heading. Odessa sank down on the sofa and started giggling to herself, then got in her car and went home--without cleaning any rooms.

Having a brilliant deductive mind (no doubt from my years at law school), I was able to imagine that there might be a connection between the disappearance of nearly a half-gallon of Cointreau and Odessa's erratic behavior. I had to give her credit, though, for picking a clear liqueur like Cointreau, where her replacing it with water could go unnoticed for weeks on the shelf. I hastened in to tell the guests that they were in fact correct, and somewhat abashed, I apologized for having stiffed them on the turndown tray.

We all had a good laugh about it, and their limousine came and whisked them away to the plantation, where no doubt the contents of the bottles of spirits were more likely to be as labeled.

A few weeks later, our children called excitedly from upstairs that the "package truck" man was heading for our door. Expecting another surprise gift for the children from their grandparents, I was surprised to find that the package was for me, and even more surprised to discover that it was a large and very expensive box of chocolates. So far as I could remember, no one was courting me--not likely after twenty years of marriage--and I could not imagine from whom the chocolates had come.

I opened the package and discovered not only a beautiful selection of handmade chocolates filled with Cointreau and Grand Marnier, but also a creamy sheet of note paper addressed to me. The handwritten inscription said "Just in case you need a reminder of how Cointreau really tastes."

Some guests have true class.

March

Springtime in Charleston is a veritable feast for the senses. The skies are bright blue, the humidity is still lingering down in the Caribbean, and every nook and cranny of our neighborhood seems to overflow with blooming things. Just walking around our block in the early evening in the spring is magical.

As you head down the block toward the water, the shafts of late afternoon sunlight illumine the ripples on the surface of the harbor and cause the crisp white sails of passing boats to glow with a pale golden warmth. The gentle breeze picks up the slightly citrusy scent of the tea olives, which mixes with the strong perfume of the wisteria vines which are thrusting impossibly large cascades of purple flowers through wrought iron fences, over walls, and down from tree limbs. Azaleas form vivid puddles of pink and fuchsia in the shadows of old brick walls covered

145

with moss, lichen, and creeping fig. If it's a Saturday, you may be treated to not only the distant beauty of St. Michael's chimes striking every quarter hour, but also a joyous peal of change ringing if there is an afternoon wedding. The bright hues of newly painted houses glow in the last rays of sun, which glint off highly polished brass door knobs and knockers and warm the old brick and Bermuda stone exteriors of other houses. The beauty of the city is at once palpable and throbbing, yet in some mysterious way out of reach and part of another time. It is no wonder that more visitors come to Charleston in the spring than at any other season.

One of the things we discovered is that spring, the season of rebirth, has hatched a multitude of house tours in Charleston as well. When I was a child, there were only two spring tours offered, which were organized by Historic Charleston Foundation and the Garden Club of Charleston. These tours drew people from all over the world, and offered a fascinating glimpse into the life of Charleston behind the high garden walls and beautifully carved entrance doors. Each tour would feature eight to ten historic homes and gardens, whose owners would make themselves scarce for a few hours while ticket holders would come in and be told about each house and its history by trained docents, who were usually Charleston ladies of a certain age. As spring tourism grew and the tours sold out on a regular basis, other groups began to realize that there was significant revenue potential in these house tours, and by the time we moved back to Charleston, there were a number of new tours offered to benefit schools, churches, arts organizations, sororities, historical societies, and even hounds for fox hunting. With all these competing tours, it was becoming more and more difficult for tour chairmen to find homeowners who were willing to let 500 strangers come wander through their houses.

As owners of a newly restored historic home, we were prime prospects for inclusion on house tours, and we were glad to oblige whenever we could. Not only was this a way that we could give back to the community, but it was also a good way to get word out about the bed and breakfast to tourists who were interested in historic homes. Before we knew it, we were committed to being included on five different tours in March. It would certainly provide us with extra incentive to keep the garden and house looking their best.

We soon learned that there had been another change in the house tour business with the proliferation of tours, which was that the pool of qualified volunteer docents who knew a Chippendale splat from Queen Anne and the difference between Imari and Canton porcelain had shrunk enormously. It's not easy to find people to volunteer to dress up and stand in someone else's house for three hours and tell tourgoers about the house and its furnishings. While there are still wonderful volunteer docents out there who are charming, well-informed, and gracious, there are also those who get cajoled into doing it at the last minute and who have had little or no preparation. This latter sort can create some very interesting situations for the homeowner.

One evening when the house was to be on tour, we had just finished hiding all our mail and clutter in a giant lawn debris bag, and had picked up my great-grandmother's vases from the florist, having delivered them there earlier to be filled with flowers appropriate to each room on tour that night, when the doorbell rang. It was time for the docents to arrive, and the woman at the door introduced herself and said she was in charge of the house and that the other docents would be there momentarily after they found a parking place. I offered to give her a quick pre-tour, which she declined, saying she already knew everything about the house, even though she had never been in it before. The better tours always contact the homeowners months in advance for a written house history, then have the docents come for a private tour with the owner, and assign which rooms each docent will handle, so that the result is that the docents are well-trained, well-informed, and know what they are going to do—unfortunately, this group was new in the tour business and had done none of these things.

I knew we were in trouble when the other docents arrived and the docent in charge gave a little welcoming address in which she pronounced the name of our house, the Hayne House, as the "Hiney House." Since "Hiney" is a crude term for one's posterior quarters and has all sorts of unsavory connotations which could be particularly problematic for a house which is also a B&B, I hastened to correct her pronunciation and to tell her that the house was named for the illustrious Hayne family, who were of Scottish extraction and pronounced their name HANE, like the stockings.

This woman drew herself up to her full height of perhaps 5' 6", pushed her glasses down her nose, glared at me, and said, "Please do NOT correct me. I am quite confident of this pronunciation, as I asked specifically about it at a meeting."

I smiled and as calmly as I could (while imagining the vice squad descending to close down any B&B that billed itself as the Hiney House) said, "I am so sorry, but I am afraid you were misinformed. The family name is Hayne, and it has always been pronounced HANE in this city. I really would prefer that you not mispronounce the name of the house."

The woman leaned forward toward me and said "It's HINEY, sir. I knew many people with this name in

Chicago before we moved down here last year after I finished cosmetology school, and all of them pronounced it HINEY, and that is what I intend to do. I would suggest that you leave and let me get on with talking to these docents."

I must admit that at this point I was getting pretty annoyed. Here I was, trying to help this organization by letting them use our house, not to mention all the special cleaning we had done and the several hundred dollars we had spent on flowers, and my reward was to be lectured at by some woman from Chicago, of all places, about how to pronounce one of the proudest names in South Carolina history, with the possible consequence of our house becoming known as the heart of Charleston's red light district.

I took some deep breaths and tried to think of what I could do quickly to solve this dilemma, as tourgoers would be arriving any minute. Finally, I had an inspiration. My friend Elizabeth Hagood is descended from the Haynes, so I ran quickly and called her on the portable phone. Fortunately, she was at home, and I said "Elizabeth, I don't have the time to explain, but I need you to pronounce the name of the Hayne family several times in an emphatic tone of voice for me when I give you the signal." Puzzled but willing to help, she agreed.

I strode into the Drawing Room, confronted Ms.

Chicago in front of the other docents, and said "On this telephone I have a direct descendant of the Hayne family who lived here who will now pronounce the name as it is pronounced by the family. Will you accept her pronunciation?"

Grudgingly, she said "I suppose so."

As I handed Ms. Chicago the phone, I said to Elizabeth "You're on" and I could soon hear the gratifying echo of Elizabeth saying "HANE....HANE....HANE..."

I took the phone from Ms. Chicago, thanked Elizabeth, and hung up. There was a loud knock at the door, and looking out the window I could see tourgoers lined up. I hastened out the back door, and as I walked up the street to the car I could hear Ms. Chicago intoning "Welcome to the third home on tonight's King Street tour, known as the Hayne House or the Hiney House, depending on who you ask."

At least I had made some progress, but I firmly resolved that this particular group would not be using our house for a tour again any time soon.

Two nights later we were scheduled to be on yet another tour. I was in somewhat of a panic because the tour was supposed to begin at 7 p.m., but here it was 6:45 and there were still no docents. This was another group that had only recently started doing house tours, and once again there had been no pre-tour or other orientation for the tour guides. Finally, at 6:50 the doorbell rang, and several college girls were there. They told me they had to do some service hours for their sorority and had been dropped off here. Did I know whether they were supposed to babysit or do something else?

I told them that I thought they were supposed to be docents in the house for the tour, and they said "Great! That sounds like fun. What's a docent?"

At this moment, the back door flew open and in walked a young woman of about 30, clad in black leather from head to toe and carrying a simply enormous stuffed monkey. She strode forward, grabbed my hand, and said, "Sorry I'm so late. My name's Trixie and I'm the head docent for the tour."

Thinking to myself that at least we didn't have Trixie here in her outfit while we were being called the Hiney House, I could not stop myself from asking "Why in the world do you have that stuffed monkey with you?"

At this point, she thrust the monkey down in one of our antique wing chairs in the Drawing Room, and in an oddly strangled voice said, "I am an amateur ventriloquist. I think people are bored with old ladies telling them about all this old furniture, so I decided I would have my MONKEY tell the tourgoers about your house. It will be something different. Don't you think it would be great?"

Thankfully, after our last tour experience disaster, I

had had the presence of mind before this tour of getting the cell phone number of the tour chairman. Grabbing my cellphone, I called and told her I was pulling the house off the tour immediately if she did not tell this docent that she was absolutely forbidden (1) to have the monkey tell people about my house and (2) to do any ventriloquism in my Drawing Room.

Fortunately, the tour chairman was as horrified as I was and said she was coming down to replace the docent right away, which she did. I am sure the tourgoers wondered what was going on as on her way out the leather-clad ventriloquist went down the line of those waiting to get into the house handing out business cards for her ventriloquism act with the monkey (*AVAILABLE FOR BIRTHDAYS, BAR MITZVAHS, & OTHER SPECIAL OCCASIONS*).

Two nights later, our house was on yet another tour. By this point, we were getting pretty burned out with all this tour business. We changed the water in the flowers and freshened them up with a little judicious clipping and awaited the arrival of the docents with fear and trembling. A very pleasant young man arrived and said he was the head docent and that the others were arriving shortly. I asked if he wanted a pre-tour, and he said no, and that they were not planning to say much about the house but rather to just let people wander through and ask questions.

I wondered to myself how they were going to answer the questions since I had given them no information, but we were on our way to a dinner party and I decided to just let it go. He then told me they would be done early because they were all going to a big bash for the tour helpers just down the street and that they would be sure to lock up the house for us if we were not back by the time they left.

The dinner party we attended was delightful and lasted until after midnight. When we returned home, we noticed the light was blinking on the answering machine. The first message was from the head docent at around 9:30 p.m:

"Mr. McGreevy, thank you so much for opening your house for us on the tour tonight. I am at the volunteer party now, but I think I left my keys at your house. Would you be so kind as to call my cell phone at (number) and let me know if you found them? Thanks."

I sent my wife to check the Drawing Room, and sure enough, there were the keys on the secretary. I tried to call the young man's cell phone, but it just rang and rang. I then proceeded to listen to the remaining two messages on the answering machine.

The second, received at 10:30 p.m. said, "Mistuh Muhgreevy, I am havin' one awesome time at the volunteer party. Any keys yet? Call me back, bud. Ciao."

154

It sounded as if our docent had been overindulging in the liquid refreshments offered at the volunteer party.

The final message, left at 11:30 p.m. said: "Heyyyy, what's happenin! Party is AWESOME. Gotta get those keys sometime. Later, dude."

Clearly, overindulgence was too kind an expression; three sheets to the wind was more like it. I tried the cell phone again to no avail, so we went on to bed, thinking that it was a mercy that this fellow did not have keys and could not drive.

Sunday morning, I went downstairs to set the table for guest breakfast, and thought it felt unusually warm. As I walked into the dining room, I was shocked to see our little side table turned over and the dining room window wide open. A plate from the table had broken and was in shattered fragments all over the floor. I did a quick inventory of the dining room and saw that all the silver was still there and that nothing else appeared to be missing.

After cleaning up the shards of shattered porcelain and doing what I could to secure the broken window, I pondered who in the world would break into our house, especially through the dining room window, which is right on King Street and extremely visible. As I wandered through the Drawing Room, I noticed the secretary chair had been moved, and then I noticed that the keys the docent had left were missing, but nothing else. We went along to church, still mystified by exactly what had happened, but when we returned home there was another message on our answering machine from the same docent which cleared everything up.

His message said he had come by during the night and (as he put it) "let himself in" to get his keys, so we didn't need to worry about them.

I am glad he thought we were so selfless that we would be worried about his keys rather than the fact that he had apparently broken into our house!

Who ever knew that having your house on tour could be so exciting? And who ever knew we would have so many wonderful adventures running a bed and breakfast?

This year of living an adventure seemed to be on its way to being one of the best years of our lives—and who knew what the next year might hold?

-Finis-

Acknowledgements

I am so very grateful for all the support from friends and family who encouraged me to write this book, not to mention all the wonderful guests and staff who made it such fun to live the B&B adventure. Although it is impossible to name everyone, there are a few people who stand out for their roles in helping this book become a reality.

Beth Webb Hart and Pringle Franklin read early iterations of the manuscript and offered invaluable advice. K. Cooper Ray of SocialPrimer also offered valuable feedback and suggestions. Preston Hipp has been a true and constant friend and support from the first day we contemplated coming back to Charleston, and has been an enormous blessing in my life. Ben Schools encouraged me and kept me accountable about finishing the manuscript, and inspired me with his perseverance.

The congregation of St. Philip's Church and the extended family of Porter-Gaud School—administration, faculty, staff, parents, and especially my students—helped convince me that my stories were worth telling and reminded me that laughter is often tonic for the soul.

Our wonderful student helpers at the B&B—Sara Bader, Ryan Lucas, Robert Bowser, Greg Walling, David Shapiro, Lauren Peterson, Jennifer Laws, and Sarah Barrett, among others—made it possible for us to enjoy running a business while at the same time having the time and energy we needed to raise our children.

Our French friends in Paris, the Daniel family and the Gotti family, gave us the great gift of sending their children Marie-Céline Daniel and Adrien and Alexandre Gotti to help us out for months at a time when we needed it the most.

Last but not least, my amazing parents, Ken and Amy McGreevy, and my tireless sister, Maribeth McGreevy Minschwaner, were faithful supporters and promoters of the B&B, as were my parents-in-law, John and Linda Whitney. We could never have done the B&B without them! And finally, my wife, Jane, and children Whit, Amy, Mary Hollis, and Anne, who lived these tales with me and have always been there with their love and support and sense of humor, will always have my deepest love and gratitude.

17920778R00095

Made in the USA
Charleston, SC
07 March 2013